4.75

# Indians:
# The Urban Dilemma

Edgar J. Dosman

P9-BIM-937

McClelland and Stewart

*The Canadian Publishers*
McClelland and Stewart Limited
25 Hollinger Road, Toronto 374

Printed and bound in Canada

# Contents

# Preface

Saskatoon, Saskatchewan is an oasis of civilization on the relentless Prairie horizon: prosperous and tidy; a melange of successful ethnic groups; tolerant, remarkably free of the more distressing fanaticisms. In spite of some poorer areas and the occasional skid row district, this Canadian city of 125,000 is emphatically a "nice" University town (even charming), a good place to raise a family, so to speak.

I remembered it for its bold attempts to compensate for the limitations of climate and geography. A farmhouse nearby shelters one of the few surviving sets of Amati string instruments in the world. The social elite of the city is extremely cosmopolitan and well-travelled (a function of the absolute requirement of periodic escape from the winter). A spirit of political creativity pervades the city.

But something had changed: the "Indian Problem" had come to town and taken the city unawares. As late as 1963, Indians were rarely seen in Saskatoon, even on the West Side, across the tracks. Some Metis families had taken residence in the city early in its century-old history, but they had long lost a consciousness of, and pride in, native ancestry. Certainly until the mid-sixties, the rather catchy Indian name "Saskatoon, Saskatchewan" evoked at best an obscure hit-parade album rather than the memory of Cree territory.

The fact was that the founding of the city coincided with the disappearance of the last vestige of Indian and Metis independence on the Canadian Plains. Indians were meant to be on reserves. And since the major Indian reserves were surveyed at some considerable distance from Saskatoon, even Indian transients were uncommon on the streets. The single small Sioux

4

reserve near the city yielded a few live-in domestics and some children were being educated away from their families in Saskatoon by 1963. But the permanent residence of registered Indians and Metis from the North was most exceptional, and stemmed mainly from the long confinements of native people in the local Tuberculosis Sanitorium.

I cannot claim any high-sounding academic reasons for this study. It began entirely by accident, impelled equally by voyeurism and a sense of moral outrage. One evening I chanced upon two City Policemen dashing to an Indian teenager, ordering him to "put them up," and then frisking him thoroughly and for no apparent reason. Without apologizing they walked back to the police car and drove away. Child's play after Boston and New York, but outrageous in Canada in general and Saskatoon in particular.

My recollections of Indians were different: digging seneca roots together shortly after the war with old car springs; a terrible sense of distance from these quiet people with their beautiful eyes; my fear of drinking out of their gallon jug of water; an incomprehensible inability to talk to an Indian boy of my age. My grandfather dismissed them as foreign, and indeed when they never returned I recalled them as being stranger even than the French in the next village. After that seneca-root season I had seen Indians only in passing.

I resolved to go Indian-hunting in Saskatoon: to note the depth of discrimination; to observe the life-style of the Indian-Metis minority in the city – family life; social life; housing; medical and welfare families; links with the reserve; work opportunities; their reasons for migrating to cities; the relationship between the urban problem and the bleak history of the native people in general; the reaction of white groups and agencies to the growth of a racial slum. I even thought for a while that I could "help" (was I not Harvard-armoured; were these not the downtrodden masses?) but that was many, many years ago.

Many people assisted at every stage of the writing of this book. Although most persons cannot be individually acknowledged here, special thanks are extended to Mr. and Mrs. John McLeod; Rodney Soonias; Valentine Nighttraveller; Arthur Turner; Susan Koch; D. Bell; Howard Adams; M. Whitehead; F. Flynn; Joan Seed; H. T. Wilson; Nancy Byers; Mrs. Valerie Bruce

5

and Stuart Raby. Officials of the Indian Affairs Branch, in particular M. B. Taylor, offered helpful advice as the research progressed. The Private and Public School Boards of the City of Saskatoon and the various Welfare Agencies similarly extended enthusiastic cooperation. It goes without saying, however, that nothing whatsoever could have been accomplished without the support of the Indian-Metis community of Saskatchewan. I am responsible for errors and other deficiencies.

E.J.D.

# Introduction:
## The Urban Dilemma

Tolerant, prosperous and smug Canada has awakened to a racial problem and is painfully adjusting to a historical sin. In the last decade, citizens, academics, and officialdom have become increasingly concerned about the condition of the half-million Indians and Metis in the country. Feeding on a new demand, the mass media have given much attention to the so-called "Indian problem." At the United Nations, Canada is regularly reminded that the treatment of its native population leaves something to be desired.

The evidence of native poverty and exclusion is so overwhelming that few observers even attempt to dispute the contention that the treatment of the native people in Canada has been a national disaster. In 1964 total earnings from gainful employment of this population amounted to $300 per capita, as compared to the Canadian average of $1,400. The incidence of diseases associated with poverty is two to three times as high for Indians and Metis as it is for whites.

In the last decade, many members of this underprivileged minority group have been migrating to cities. According to the *Hawthorn Report – A Survey of the Contemporary Indians of Canada: A Report on Economic, Political and Educational Needs and Policies*, requested by the Department of Citizenship and Immigration in 1964 and published in October 1966: "At the present rate of population growth, a critical phase of this movement could be reached in ten years' time, even if the reserves continue to hold the present numbers. Problems of housing, placement, recreation and training will be intensified and in many ways will be special to the Indians."[1]

Indeed the federal policy of "termination" as outlined in a

*White Paper* of July 1969, would intensify the out-migration of Indians. It proposes to eliminate Indian 'special status,' thereby depopulating the reserves and driving occupants into urban centres.[2]

Available data on Indian-Metis migration to Canadian cities suggest an even more rapid rate of urbanization than the *Hawthorn Report* had anticipated. The James Smith Reserve, in northern Saskatchewan, would appear to give a typical pattern: 250 persons out of a population of 931 were living off the reserve in 1968, as against 160 out of 914 in 1967, and 26 out of 830 in 1965. Over a quarter of Canadian Indians now live off the reserve.[3] The majority of the Indian population will inexorably shift to the cities.

The appearance of Indian poverty in Canadian cities has produced unprecedented problems. Native people form the hard core of the urban dispossessed: almost the entire minority lies outside the socio-economic structure of the city. The Indian subculture is not merely low in status and income; it is not merely at the bottom of the pile; its situation is becoming increasingly worse.

Yet the observer is struck by the large number of official and voluntary services designed to *assist* the native people in adjusting to urban life. Some programs, federal and provincial, are designed specifically for Indians and Metis as a specially disadvantaged group. Others, by far in the majority, extend welfare and related services available to all citizens. These services will collectively be labelled *poverty programs*.

The single most striking characteristic of the Indian-Metis minority in the city is the extent to which it is manipulated by and dependent on these bureaucratic services. The poverty programs mediate between the white and Indian subsystems; they distribute scarce resources; and they control the information network regarding employment, housing and welfare; they punish and reward. They do not merely *affect* the adjustment process of the individual native person entering the city; they are an intrinsic part of the dynamic shaping of the ethnic stratification system itself.

The purpose of the book is to study the apparent failure, so far, of attempts to arrest the growth of Indian poverty in Canadian cities. I am increasingly convinced that the already vast and rapidly growing social welfare establishment surrounding the "urban Indian problem" operates programs that are misdirected;

that administrators perceive only a part of a complex reality; that they design programs using the wrong models; and that they thereby intensify the prevailing maladjustment. After a decade of experience it is time to take stock of an urgent social issue and reassess the future of official and voluntary efforts designed to facilitate the adjustment of the Indians and Metis to the urban environment.

At this stage, the most pressing need is still to elaborate the problem. Although there is a vast anthropological literature on the North American Indian, the contributions of scholars and government agencies to an understanding of Indians in the urban situation have not been impressive. In most cities the native population is already so large and anonymous, and the level of hostility to whites so great, that effective discourse on this subject is out of the question. Indians and Metis associate sociologists with social workers and policemen. I have therefore chosen to describe racial relations in one city, where racial hostility is still fairly low and where the population is of a manageable size.

Saskatoon, Saskatchewan is such a city. Unusually favourable conditions permitted an intimate knowledge of Indian organizations, official agencies, voluntary programs, patterns of migration, and the dynamics of native-white interaction in general. To be sure, there are enormous differences among bands, tribes, regions, and cities in Canada; there is a danger of generalizing beyond the evidence, based as it is on a single population. The argument is simply that the benefits of this approach outweigh the costs. A thorough understanding of the problem in one city is more valuable at this point than the necessarily more superficial findings from a variety of urban centres in the country.

By the early 1960s, several factors coincided to initiate a large-scale migration of Indians and Metis into Saskatoon: an industrial and housing boom in the city which provided extensive employment opportunities; the gradual awakening of Indians to possibilities outside the reserves in the larger cities; the greater access of the native population to transportation facilities; and the breakdown of the controls previously exercised over the Indians by the Indian Affairs Branch. The most important development, however, has been the rapid population increase of Indians and Metis in Canada in general. In the province of Saskatchewan, with a population of less than a million, the proportion of native people is very large, over 8 per cent, with a birth rate about *three* times that of the white population. Since

9

1958, the native population has doubled, placing tremendous pressure on the reserves (and on the nerves of the white majority). The same is true of the Metis population in their impoverished communities: local resources cannot possibly sustain the burgeoning families.

The city of Saskatoon itself is a natural choice for relocation. It is the nearest large centre in the province for migrating Indians and Metis from the North. It promises employment, educational opportunities, and recreation. By 1969, a sizeable Indian-Metis minority of over 2,000 had entrenched itself in the city; two years later it had already doubled in size.

The native minority, therefore, is largely first generation, but it has already developed a very distinctive social structure and life-style, bearing little resemblance to that of the larger society.

The characteristic feature of the group in Saskatoon, looked at as a whole, is associated with skid row. Indeed, the Indians' move to the city is a case history of an urban slum-in-making. *Some* members of other ethnic groups have also failed to adjust to urban life, and have fallen into more or less permanent welfare dependency. The "poverty wall" surrounds not only Indians but millions of white Canadians as well. But *most* Indians in the city are in this predicament. When this happens, a *quantitative* difference becomes *qualitative*.

But an equally striking characteristic of the native minority is the role and position in urban life of those Indians who have adjusted to relocation. An important segment has adapted very well to the new environment. Moreover, other Indians and Metis are engaged in a heroic struggle to keep off the welfare rolls. There appear to be, in fact, three distinct "classes" or groupings within the native community in the city, each with different backgrounds and problems. The dilemma of Indian poverty in the city cannot be understood unless this stratification system is dissected.

## Methodology

The present study is directed toward the discovery and delineation of socio-cultural variables which determine the adaptation process in the special culture-change situation of the urban environment. As such it would appear to lend itself to refined survey techniques and in-depth interviews. In the case of Indians and Metis, however, it is not possible to conduct a scientifically valuable survey based on long questionnaires, or to interview a large or representative sample of the major Indian-Metis groupings in the city. Those days, if they ever existed, are gone. After a century of ruthless analysis, Indians are unanimous in their rejection of surveys, whether conducted by Whites or Indians. Native people are about as willing to confide in an interviewer as the average Catholic is to divulge secrets of the Confessional.

Information, therefore, had to be assembled in less direct ways: participant observation; intensive family studies; unstructured conversations; and association with Indian organizations, official agencies, and native-white action programs. The spatial distribution of the native population in the city, and a large and representative number of complete case studies, were drawn together from archives, welfare rolls, employment records, and job placement files; the careful assessment of patterns of communication was built up from information collected by Indian-Metis organizations in the city; the study of reserve kinship structures was made possible by the cooperation of interested native people. The bulk of the data was collected in 1968-1969. The quality of the data obtained with the active and intensive cooperation of native and white associates ensured the possibility of transcending an arbitrary reporting of random observations.

Some definitional and other qualifications are in order. Despite the legal and administrative distinctions between Indians and Metis, the term "Indian" will refer to the entire indigenous population, except where specifically indicated. The differences are very significant in some cases, but in the city both groups, given their similar origins and racial appearance, are confronted by a common exclusion from white society.

According to the *Indian Act*, registered Indians include all persons descended in the male line from a paternal ancestor of Indian identity, who have chosen to remain under Indian legislation.[4] The term "Metis" (mixed blood) is most adequately defined operationally as 'people who share a consciousness of Metis peoplehood.' Although their indigenous status has been recognized by various governments at one time or another, Metis are officially seen by Ottawa as just another of Canada's minority groups, and they are not governed by a special hierarchy of officials.[5] Nevertheless, to the larger society, somebody who looks 'Indian' is an Indian. Discussion of family and class in the present essay will rely heavily on the experience of treaty Indians rather than Metis. Consistent with the definition of Indian as given, the Metis are not considered to be excluded from the discussion, although occasionally, they will be specifically indicated.

Second, the process of migration and urbanization which I describe cannot be extended to those communities or situations where whites are in a minority or near-minority position. There are typologies available of culture-clash situations in Canada and the United States, and there is no necessity to duplicate those efforts.

The 'urban environment' as I define it extends to the centres of 100,000 or above. Despite the significant variations from one end of the country to the other, my guess is that in life-style and social structure, the Saskatoon Indians are representative of the urbanization process in the country.

Finally, as an explanatory word, the book is written for social planners and the general public as well as for students and colleagues. As a result, theoretical discussion has been kept to a minimum, and other canons of academic research have been compromised, if not altogether violated. In particular, I have generally withstood the temptation to relate my findings to those of other writers, except where such digression was crucial to clarify the issue in question.

On the other hand, while the subject matter of the book necessitates digging into dark corners, I have not washed dirty linen in public for its own sake. The Indian tragedy exposes the bleakest side of Canadian civilization; it does not rule out the possibility of reform. My purpose here is twofold: to describe the life-style of the native community, and to relate it to its unique historical development in Canadian society as a whole.

---

[1] Canada, Department of Indian Affairs and Northern Development, Indian Affairs Branch. *A Survey of the Contemporary Indians of Canada: A Report in Economic, Political and Educational Needs and Policies.* H. B. Hawthorn, ed., 2 vols., Ottawa, Queen's Printer, 1966.

[2] Canada, Department of Indian Affairs and Northern Development, Indian Affairs Branch, Technical Services Division. *Reserve Population Statistics.*

[3] Department of Indian Affairs and Northern Development. *The New Indian Policy*, Ottawa, July, 1969.

[4] Canada. *The Indian Act as Amended*, 1961, Ottawa, Queen's Printer, 1965.

[5] Although the Metis were not given special legislative status, the Government of Canada granted them special treatment in the administration of federal lands. Both Metis children and heads of families were given a choice between a payment of money or land for the extrication of the Indian title. (See M. Giraud, "The Western Metis After the Insurrection," *Saskatchewan History*, vol. 9, No. 1, winter 1956, p. 2.)

# 1
## Genesis

*All that the native has seen in his country is that they can freely arrest him, beat him, starve him: and no professor of ethics, no priest has ever come to be beaten in his place, nor to share their bread with him.* [*Frantz Fanon*]

The life of an Indian was never isolated from *all* contacts with white society, only from *most*. He was numbered and rationed, and closely watched. He could do almost nothing without the permission of the Indian Agent: buy or sell; slaughter cattle; be educated; drink or travel. While every person of whatever background relates to his primary group of family and peers, his community and the outside world, Indians have an exceptional balance, or rather imbalance, among these levels. The outside world, the Indian Affairs framework, not only determined the Indian's income, living conditions, education and mobility; it also made every attempt to shape his culture and personality. It is for this reason that a study of Canadian Indians must start, not with "culture," or the "culture of poverty," but with the institutions that dominated him and the society that destroyed him.

### Annihilation

The coming of the settler to Western Canada introduced a sharp differentiation both physically and culturally between the indigenous and white populations. This was not always the case in the period prior to the settlement of the West. When the economy of Western Canada was largely nomadic, based on the river and forest, and when the buffalo herds provided sufficient food for the Indian bands, there was, for example, considerable cooperation between white residents of the Hudson's Bay Company and

13

the Indian and Metis traders and trappers. Unquestionably the introduction of an alien culture into these areas undermined the traditional culture of the Indian bands, but the Metis in particular, "that invaluable class of men," mediating between the aborigines and the first settlers, constituted a bridge across the "gulf of ignorance, misunderstanding, fear and clashing interests that created the havoc of Indian wars south of the border."[1]

But the mass influx of settlers changed all that; both the Metis and the Indians, following the disappearance of the buffalo, were ground down into a miserable dependent existence. By the 1870s in the West, there was no alternative for the Indians: they had to salvage whatever they could in an enforced settlement with the Canadian Government. The Indians, therefore, "took treaty."

> Early in the settlement of North America, the British recognized an Indian title or interests in the soil to be parted with or extinguished by agreement with the Indians and then only to the Crown. This gave rise to the practice of making agreements or treaties, as they were afterwards called, with various Indian tribes. The policy began in British colonial times in what is now the United States and was afterwards introduced into Canada. As settlement began in Southern Ontario, treaties were made with the Indians for their surrender of their interest in the land. In return, the Crown undertook to set aside reserves and provide additional facilities and other considerations. In regard to Indians not already dealt with, Canada followed the policy of making treaties after Confederation, beginning in Manitoba and northwestern Ontario, continuing on throughout the major part of the West and Northwest and then back again to include all of Northern Ontario. About half the Indian population of Canada is under treaty; the Indians of Quebec, the Maritimes, British Columbia, the Iroquois and certain other groups who emigrated from the United States being excluded.[2]

Although after Confederation jurisdiction for Indian Affairs was vested in the Government of Canada, it never found a really comfortable niche in the federal Government machinery. At first the Department of the Secretary of State was given jurisdiction but by 1873 it had already been shifted to the Department of the Interior. In 1880, a separate Department of Indian Affairs was established. In 1936, Indian Affairs again became a Branch, this time of the Ministry of Mines and Resources. In 1950 the Department of Citizenship and Immigration took it, and in 1966, it became a Branch of the Department of Indian Affairs and Northern Development.

By the terms of the *Indian Act*, Indians are wards of the state, and the authority of the Indian Affairs Branch extended into the most minute details of the lives of individual Indians. Administration was carried on through a headquarters staff at Ottawa as well as agencies in the field responsible for one or more reserves and bands. In turn, the work of the agencies was (and remains) supervised by regional supervisors. The management of the reserves, education, the administration of band funds, relief, descent of property, Indian treaty obligation, welfare projects, enfranchisement of Indians – in short, an enormous range of responsibilities was given over to the Indian Affairs Branch.

According to the Hawthorn Report:

> ... Indian Administration was a version of colonialism. The Branch was a quasi-colonial government dealing with almost the entire life of a culturally different people who were systematically deprived of opportunities to influence government, a people who were isolated on separate pockets of land and who were subject to different laws.[3]

The Indian reserves were segregated from the larger society; indeed, on the Prairies the Indian Agents maintained a strict watch over the movements of the Indians off the reserves, and even between reserves.

> The policy aimed to settle the natives on reserved areas where their abode would be fixed and permanent; to abate and transform the annual distribution of 'presents' (gifts of making treaty, or annuities), which of all things, wrongfully encouraged the Indians to regard the government as a bountiful source of continuing generosity; and to civilize and Christianize the natives into conformity with the rest of the population. This would be a new kind of peace in which the settler would have the land and be able to work it without fear of interference. Once these became the ends of govern-

15

ment, the concept of *administration* was born; the government had ceased to deal with the Indians as allies and had
imposed the status of wardship.[4]

The reports of the North West Mounted Police from their
various commands in the then-Northwest Territories quite openly
viewed the Indians as an occupied people. Nothing is more
characteristic of the general attitude toward the Indians than the
constant nonchalant accounts of disasters, tragedies, and epidem-
ics striking the Indian population, without so much as a hint of
regret at these events. The *Agent Reports* bristle with comments
typical of the bloated European racism of the late Nineteenth
Century ("blood savage," and the like).

Patrols swept through the reserves at regular intervals to
assure protection for the settlers and their cattle. The police gave
every possible assistance to return "deserters" from the industrial
schools in the various districts; they also aided the Agent and the
Church in suppressing Indian customs that inhibited the virtues
of farming and self-support. Similarly, it was the duty of the
police to make sure that Indians had passes when they left the
reserve, and generally to keep close watch on them.[5]

As harsh as police administration may have been, and as
clear the lines of division between Indian and white culture, there
is every reason to suspect that the Indians would have fared
much worse at the hands of the settlers without the presence of
the police. The Canadian settlers shared the expansionist urge
and land hunger of the Europeans that spread throughout North
and South America, Australia, and parts of Africa. There is an
ironic validity to the IAB comment that "firmness, fair dealing,
courage, and kindness had their effect and next to the Indian
Affairs Branch itself, the Indians throughout Canada never had
better or more valuable friends than the Mounties."[6]

In the mid-nineteenth century, the French writer, Alexis de
Tocqueville, gave a first and brilliant analysis of the treatment
afforded the Indians by the white settlers in America. Although
impressed by the overall vigour of political life in the United
States, he lamented the cruelty of the New World peoples in the
treatment of Indians and Blacks. Whereas the Spanish had tried
to exterminate the indigenous population and failed, the Americans and Australians very largely succeeded, not so much by
conscious mass killings (although that occurred regularly as well)
as by the total and rapid undermining of the native culture:

16

The Spaniards, by unparalleled atrocities which brand them with indelible shame, did not succeed in exterminating the Indian race and could not even prevent them from sharing their rights; the United States Americans have attained both these results with wonderful ease; quietly, legally and philanthropically, without spilling blood and without violating a single one of the great principles of morality in the eyes of the world. It is impossible to destroy men with more respect for the laws of humanity.[7]

It is true that extermination was not so much a feature of the Canadian West as it was in many of the Indian Wars in the United States. That much the North West Mounted Police prevented. Indeed, the Sioux sought refuge in Canada, and some bands took permanent residence north of the 49th Parallel. Instead of being exterminated, the Indians were shoved off into reserves.[8] A minimal morality also asserted itself in allotting a few tax monies to a derelict indigenous population, but it kept them apart – hidden and totally powerless.

Whether the European fragment destroys, isolates or incorporates the aborigine, the record is vivid with bloodshed. Here is the ironic compensation it experiences for leaving its enemies in Europe behind, that it meets even stronger antagonisms abroad. Its encounter brings out all of the hidden values shared with others in the Old Country, its basic Europeanism, and in doing so it unleashes a violent energy that transcends even that which produced the guillotine of the Old World.[9]

In Western Canada, the confrontation between the settler and the native population was no more brutal than was necessary to achieve the goal of the settlers: a contractual society underwritten by the common norms of European experience. The overwhelming power of the State implemented the objective, sweeping away the culture which stood in its path.

For all of the differences among the various ethnic groups that settled Western Canada, they agreed about the question of the native population which lay outside their consensus of values. They accepted the reserves, but no tolerance was shown to "Indianness" outside them. This is shown clearly in the terms of the treaties. When the various chiefs suggested in their talks with

Governor Morris that the Indians be permitted some exceptions in the settler society because of their inexperience in handling money, they were invariably turned down. Every time that the issue came up, Governor Morris objected that such exceptions would interfere with private enterprise. "It is unlikely," he said, regarding the building of bridges for the Indians, "that the Government will build any. They prefer to leave it to private enterprise to do these things."[10]

White society was not to be compromised in any way. The candid *Annual Reports* of the Indian Agents forcefully indicate their perseverance in attempts to civilize the Indians into accepting the capitalist settler economy. The curriculum enforced by the Indian affairs administration extolled the value of patriotism and self-support. Knowledge of English was stressed. "Ethics" included:

> The practice of cleanliness, obedience, respect, order, neatness. . . . Right and wrong. Truth. Continuance of proper appearance and behaviour. . . . Patriotism. Evils of Indian isolation. Enfranchisement. Labour the law of life. Relations of the sexes as to labour. Home and public duties.[11]

The political event which most clearly revealed the intrinsic separatism between the native population and the white settlers was the Riel Rebellion of 1885, and the subsequent physical extermination of Louis Riel for his sin of native pride. It was the last flicker of independence among the Indian-Metis groups in Saskatchewan, although it is clear that there was little coordination among the various native factions.[12] The essence of the situation was the incompatibility of a dominant white society and a fading native culture. Chief Big Bear, who took part in the Rebellion, realized that the Indians would suffer psychological annihilation on the reserves. Riel wanted a great many things, among them the right of the Metis nation to negotiate genuinely with the Canadian Government for legitimate claims based on its indigenous status. After 1885, the vast majority of the Metis who could not adapt sank into a miserable existence clustered around the Indian reserves deep in the wilds of the Northlands. The treaty Indians had no alternative to reserve life.

Following the Riel Rebellion, the reserve policy was so triumphantly successful that the native population was almost completely forgotten. The reserve system practically eliminated the Indians from intercourse with white society; the conscience of the settlers was appeased in direct proportion to the invisibility of the savages. The experience of the Metis was altogether as severe as that of the Indians, even though the administrative structure was different. The unadaptable Metis were excluded from the white society and made totally dependent on it.

The colonial experience of the Indian population – its fundamental similarity to the experience of other colonized peoples – forms the essential point of departure for the analysis of Indian-white relations in Canada. Even the *Hawthorn Report* places great emphasis on the comparison of the Indian population with the emergent peoples in the "Third World." The exclusion of the Indians was meant to be as complete as possible, admitting only those Indians who were fully prepared to be assimilated into the white society. So insistent was this policy of exclusion that the federal franchise was not extended to Indians until 1960, and in many provinces the provincial vote was withheld nearly as long. Given the history of cultural contact, the results were predictable:

> For many Indians the accumulation of political exclusion and a special system of administration came to be psychologically coupled with a lack of identification with the political system of the larger society, and with a tenacious emphasis on their own unique status. The extent of this was dramatically revealed when the extension of the federal and provincial franchise met with little popular acclaim, much suspicion and occasional hostility.[13]

### The Strategy of Assimilation

The *objectives* of the Indian Affairs Branch are clear enough: assimilation. Officials until recently were not embarrassed to be frank about it. Thus the *Indian Acts* of 1868-1869 were described by the Deputy Superintendent General as being "designed to lead the Indian people by degrees to mingle with the white race in the ordinary avocations of life."[14] Another stated that "the happiest future for the Indian race is absorption into the general population and this is the policy of [the] government."[15] As late as 1961, an official IAB publication envisioned the extinction of Indians as *Indians* in a mortifying homily:

> The old Indian culture will inevitably be absorbed by ours, but it will never be forgotten, and the Indian contribution to

19

our civilization will remain of great value. In . . . corn, beans, squash, artichokes, sunflowers and tobacco, to say nothing of potatoes from further south, we have gained far more than all the gold the Spaniards have looted from the Indies.[16]

The apparent contradiction between a policy of assimilation and the maintenance of the reserves therefore dissolves. The reserves were meant to serve as forcing grounds for the inculcation of "white" values and religion, until the Indian could be assimilated into the larger society. The strictness of reserve control (the pass system was abolished only in the 1930's) was designed to protect the Indian Affairs Branch's program of "citizen apprenticeship" from premature and debilitating contact with white society.

First, both Church and State cooperated in a guerrilla war on Indian culture, for both believed in the coincidence of assimilation and Christianity. A later anti-clerical age is likely to be morally outraged by so advanced a form of Christian righteousness, particularly the blatant attempt to suppress Indian religion and ritual; but it encompasses in general the obvious alliance between Church and State in Indian administration:

The missionaries are a part of the standing army of our Dominion who . . . help to maintain the peace and prosperity of our land . . . prepare the districts for the advent of the settler. . . . It pays to send the Gospel to the Indians.[17]

In education, considered by the Indian Affairs Branch to be the key to the improvement of the situation, great emphasis was placed on isolating promising Indian youths from the influence of the reserve.

The Indian youth, to enable him to cope successfully with his brother of white origin, must be disassociated with the prejudicial influences by which he is surrounded on the reserve of his band. And the necessity for the establishment of general institutions, where Indian children, besides being instructed in the usual branches of education will be lodged, fed, clothed, kept separate from home influences, taught trades and instructed in agriculture, is becoming every year more apparent.[18]

However, within the limitations of their ideology, the Churches

20

unquestionably mitigated the barbarisms that would have been inflicted on the native population by the grasping settlers. This is even more true of the Metis than the Indians after the treaties and the Northwest Rebellion of 1885. The Federal Commission established on March 31, 1885, to deal with Metis claims following the Revolt, applied the principles that had been followed in Manitoba. To Metis children born before July 15, 1870, there was a choice offered between "scrip" valued at $240.00 (negotiable or to be used for the purchase of federal lands); and a land scrip which authorized a choice of 240 acres of unoccupied Dominion land. Heads of families could also choose between these two kinds of scrip but their respective values were $160.00 or 160 acres.[19]

**Graph 1**

**Indian population in Canada**
**Ten year intervals 1924 to December 31, 1967**

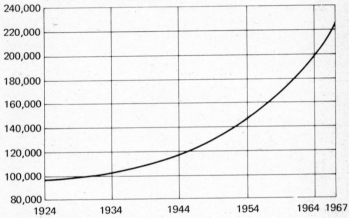

From the point of view of a white settler, these were not inconsiderable benefits, provided they were carefully saved and invested. They admitted the indigenous status of the Metis people by a privileged treatment in the administration of federal lands. They were not, however, made wards of the State as were the Indian bands. Yet the results were disastrous.[20] The Metis simply were not able to hold their ground in competition with the white settlers. The missionaries were most concerned about them to the extent of attempting to establish a Metis reserve to protect a poverty-stricken and wandering people helpless against white society, and excluded from the reserves. Thus Giraud comments that: "It was indeed the missionaries alone who made any serious attempt at coming to the assistance of the Metis group, or at least rescuing them from their steady downfall."[21]

The attempt to set up a reserve in 1896 failed, leaving the Churches with the alternative only of protecting the more promising Metis: getting them into an Indian reserve, even if the letter of the law had to be transgressed. This was a process distinct from intermarriage with Metis women from the shacks in the road allowance around the reserves; or from the intermarriage between Indians and Metis who were allowed into the treaties. Promising Metis married to notable Indians could serve a purpose on the reserve which the IAB could not but approve. In many agricultural areas in Saskatchewan, the Metis on the reserves were efficient farmers, models of self-support for the Indians. They were also often lighter-skinned, "whiter" so to speak, a fact of no small importance, as amply demonstrated by the chuckles of Agents and missionaries.[22]

The strategy of assimilation now becomes clear. Both Church and State singled out the most promising families on the reserves as candidates for eventual "enfranchisement" (as the legal renunciation of Indianness has been termed). Both Agents and local priests and ministers fostered a special clientele group of successful Indian farmers who, they hoped, would be progressively weaned away from their Indian heritage into an acceptance of white norms. The Churches had a monopoly on education; the Indian Affairs Branch a monopoly on money and power. Together they formed an unbeatable combination, and could make or break Indians at will. Agents' Reports to Ottawa continually underlined the success they were having in encouraging specific families to be more thrifty, to grow more produce, to enlarge their gardens and to go to Church more regularly. Similarly Churchmen jealously guarded Indian seminary recruits and bright boys who took an interest in the Ministry.

By the same token, the "leading families" sponsored by the Indian Affairs Branch and the Church would create a group of "brokers" on the reserve who could mediate between the Agent and Minister on the one hand, and the less acculturated reserve Indians on the other. As a system of indirect rule, it greatly assisted governing reserves, giving a fig-leaf of legitimacy to

22

Government dictates. The similarity of this strategy with colonial policies elsewhere is obvious.

Essentially there has been no self-government on Indian reserves. The significance of this extraordinary state of affairs can be seen by comparisons with white communities.[23] The latter are located within the provincial structure of local government; municipal institutions perform many important services in the areas of health, education and welfare; and local governments in return receive heavy financial support from the Provinces for administering these services.

Yet Indians have been historically outside this structure of local government. The Indian Affairs Branch directly administered the reserves like private fiefdoms, with a full range of health, welfare and education programs of their own. Needless to say, there has been an inevitable tendency toward increasing cooperation with provincial and local governments in the dispensing of these services. For a century, however, the individual reserve was an isolated pocket of direct rule from Ottawa. The special nature of Indian communities, particularly in community membership and property ownership, further differentiates Indian from non-Indian communities.[24]

However, the *Indian Act* did provide for a formal instrument of local self-government on reserves: the *band council*. In the past decade some band councils have gained greater control over their own affairs. But for a century, the band councils were rubber stamps for the rules laid down by the Indian Affairs Branch. The band council, in short, was the officially recognized body with which the Indian Agent dealt in his dealings with the band.[25] The Indians had no say in the setting-up of this political system and the Chief and Councillors of the band council were chosen "according to the customs of the band," that is, by the Indian Agent. There is no clearer symptom of colonialism than the coopting of a native elite. In this case the "leading families" were created and sustained by the Indian Affairs Branch in return for cooperation on the band councils.

Assimilation was to be mediated through these families; civilization would radiate out from these relatively prosperous groups. In turn, the intermarriage of sons and daughters from different reserves would cement friendships between the brokerage groups across the province. But no chances were taken: in case of doubt Indians were kept in the reserves where they remained under Government inspection and control. Reserve histories amply

# Saskatchewan: Location of Indian Population (key to numbering opposite)

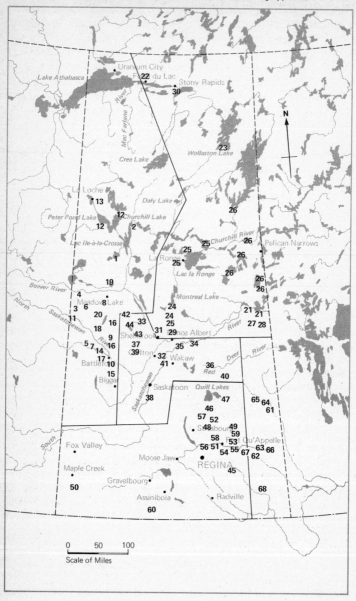

Lake Athabasca
Uranium City
Fond du Lac 22
Stony Rapids
30

Max Farlane River

Wollaston Lake 23
Cree Lake

La Loche
13
Daly Lake
Peter Pond Lake 12 12 Churchill Lake
12 2
Lac Ile-à-la-Crosse
1
26
La Ronge 25 25 Churchill River
25 Pelican Narrows 26
26
26 Lac la Ronge 26
26
26
Beaver River 19
Meadow Lake 8 Montreal Lake
4 24
North 20 24 21 21
3 6 16 33 25 27 28
11 18 44 43 31 29 ince Albert River
9 16 37 35 34
5 7 14 39 Shellbrook
17 olton 32 Wakaw Deer River
Battleford 10 41 36
15 40 Red
Biggar
Saskatoon Quill Lakes 65 64
38 47 61
46
57 52
S lsbourg 49
48 59
58 Fort Qu'Appelle 63 66
Fox Valley 56 51 53 67 62
Moose Jaw 54 55
Maple Creek REGINA 45
Gravelbourg
68
Assiniboia Radville
50
60

N

0   50   100
Scale of Miles

**Table 1**
**Indian Population of Saskatchewan by District and Band**

| | | Band Total | | | | Band Total |
|---|---|---|---|---|---|---|
| **North Battleford District** | | | | **37** Mistawasis | | 649 |
| **1** Canoe Lake | | 364 | | **38** Moose Woods | | 156 |
| **2** English River | | 396 | | **39** Muskeg Lake | | 481 |
| **3** Island Lake | | 332 | | **40** Nut Lake | | 864 |
| **4** Joseph Bighead | | 255 | | **41** One Arrow | | 429 |
| **5** Little Pine | | 590 | | **42** Pelican Lake | | 300 |
| **6** Loon Lake | | 395 | | **43** Sandy Lake | | 924 |
| **7** Lucky Man | | 39 | | **44** Witchekan Lake | | 155 |
| **8** Meadow Lake | | 248 | | | | |
| **9** Moosomin | | 472 | | District Total | | 7,375 |
| **10** Mosquito-Grizzly | | | | | | |
| Bear's Head | | 406 | | | | |
| **11** Onion Lake | | 1,174 | | **Touchwood-File Hills-** | | |
| **12** Peter Pond Lake | | 453 | | **Qu'Appelle District** | | |
| **13** Portage La Loche | | 256 | | **45** Carry the Kettle | | 755 |
| **14** Poundmaker | | 478 | | **46** Day Star | | 215 |
| **15** Red Pheasant | | 545 | | **47** Fishing Lake | | 495 |
| **16** Saulteaux | | 360 | | **48** Gordon | | 908 |
| **17** Sweet Grass | | 531 | | **49** Little Black Bear | | 159 |
| **18** Thunderchild | | 721 | | **50** Maple Creek | | 123 |
| **19** Waterhen Lake | | 501 | | **51** Muscowpetung | | 430 |
| **20** General List | | 5 | | **52** Muskowekwan | | 512 |
| | | | | **53** Okanese | | 162 |
| District Total | | 8,521 | | **54** Pasqua | | 523 |
| | | | | **55** Peepeekisis | | 771 |
| **Prince Albert District** | | | | **56** Piapot | | 653 |
| **21** Cumberland House | | 210 | | **57** Poorman | | 813 |
| **22** Fond du Lac | | 580 | | **58** Standing Buffalo | | 519 |
| **23** Lac La Hache | | 241 | | **59** Star Blanket | | 153 |
| **24** Montreal Lake | | 970 | | **60** Wood Mountain | | 71 |
| **25** Lac La Ronge | | 2,099 | | | | |
| **26** Peter Ballantyne | | 1,577 | | District Total | | 7,262 |
| **27** Red Earth | | 400 | | | | |
| **28** Shoal Lake | | 205 | | | | |
| **29** Sioux Wahpaton | | 86 | | **Yorkton District** | | |
| **30** Stony Rapids | | 494 | | **61** Côté | | 1,156 |
| **31** Sturgeon Lake | | 721 | | **62** Cowessess | | 1,056 |
| | | | | **63** Kahkewistahaw | | 498 |
| District Total | | 7,583 | | **64** Keeseekoose | | 686 |
| | | | | **65** Key | | 348 |
| **Saskatoon District** | | | | **66** Ochapowace | | 458 |
| **32** Beardy's and | | | | **67** Sakimay | | 524 |
| Okemasis | | 849 | | **68** White Bear | | 958 |
| **33** Big River | | 815 | | | | |
| **34** James Smith | | 1,025 | | District Total | | 5,684 |
| **35** John Smith | | 419 | | | | |
| **36** Kinistino | | 309 | | **Saskatchewan Total** | | 36,425 |

Department of Statistics Division, Department of Indian Affairs and
Northern Development, August 27, 1971.

25

demonstrate this strategy and its effectiveness, for government policy was successful in developing a cadre of "leading families" that responded to Indian Affairs Branch (IAB) initiatives. As later chapters will show, this reserve stratification system was not confined to the reserves, but has exercised profound influence on the native community in the urban environment.

## The Revolution in Indian Affairs

Although it is not possible to identify the specific moment at which the existing structure of Indian administration became intolerable in Canada, the years between 1960 and 1964 witnessed the moral collapse of the old order. In 1964, the Government gave expression to this general realization by requesting a comprehensive study of the situation as a basis for thorough-going reform.[26] From that time, the Indian problem has been in the forefront of the various national causes; it has led to spiralling plans and polemics, climaxed by the Government's *New Policy* of July 1969, which outlined a policy of termination.[27]

Paradoxically, the revolution in Indian affairs was at least partially precipitated by a steady advance in programs and expenditures by the Indian Affairs Branch, and the inclusion of Indians and Metis in an increasing number of provincial services. In 1958-59, the Indian Affairs Branch numbered 3500. By 1967-68, it had increased to over 8500. The cost of child maintenance and protection services increased by over 100 per cent in the years 1960-61 to 1966-67. The social assistance program expanded somewhat less rapidly but averaged close to 8 per cent in the total number of recipients between the years 1962-63 and 1966-67. In terms of actual dollar outlay the increase was on the order of 65 per cent. Before 1950 in the Saskatchewan region, the Indian Affairs Branch built 494 houses on the reserves. In contrast, in the years 1961-1970, 2224 houses were constructed.[28] The provision of massive assistance to the Indian population of Canada is now an accepted fact.

Between 1951 and 1961, federal expenditures in Indian education grew from 7.4 million dollars to 27.7 million, and school enrolment increased from 25,000 to 43,000. At the beginning of this period there were only 2,000 Indian students attending provincial schools, the others being in residential schools "operated on behalf of the Government by the churches," and in Indian day schools on the reserves. By 1961, there were over 11,000 in provincial schools. In that year the Minister could assert that "no

Indian child is denied the opportunity of education through lack of funds on the part of his parents." Branch outlays grew from $36,390,000 in fiscal 1958-59 to $41,457,555 in fiscal 1960-61. According to the Minister, "the administration of Indian affairs is now big business."[29]

A final *Report of the Joint Parliamentary Committee on Indian Affairs*, published in 1961 during John Diefenbaker's second Government, issued two recommendations: "that Government should direct more authority and responsibility to Band Councils and individual Indians with a consequent limitation of ministerial authority and control"; and that "Indian affairs should be the subject of a Dominion-Provincial Conference in order that such matters may be transferred to provincial administration as may be mutually acceptable to the Indian people, provincial and federal authorities."[30] By 1964, considerable progress had been made in both areas. Ministerial reports strongly supported the principle of increasing self-government on the reserve as well as increasing cooperation with the provinces in matters affecting education, employment, social welfare and community development. As early as 1960, the majority of Indian bands had municipal-type councils elected for two years. Five bands accepted the right to spend their own funds, "as distinct from capital expenditures, still managed by the IAB," and appointed treasurers and auditors. Others appointed welfare officers, constables, recreation directors, health and sanitation and school committees. In Saskatchewan in 1969, 51 of the 67 bands had school committees, and there were 81 full-time employees of bands.[31]

In 1960 Minister Ellen Fairclough declared that "in the field of social integration education is undoubtedly the key"; she left no doubt that her Government supported the increased enrolment of Indian children in provincial schools. Considerable publicity was given to projects where there was cooperation between the IAB and provincial governments. Thus during the construction of the International Nickel Mine and Smelter at Thompson in northern Manitoba, much headline space was given to the employment of 187 Indians and Metis out of a total of 500 workers. Questions of jurisdictions were involved, but an *ad hoc* arrangement was worked out to satisfy both provincial and IAB authorities. "In the fall the provincial Government stationed a community development officer at the site. By mutual agreement the Indian Affairs representative is to look after employment matters while the provincial man takes care of social and community development."[32]

In the Province of Saskatchewan, the late Premier W. Ross Thatcher dramatized the Indian problem by the creation of an Indian-Metis Branch (IMB) in the Department of Natural Resources in 1966 and raising it to the status of a full department in 1969. But an earlier Government, The Cooperative Commonwealth Federation (CCF), had also become somewhat aware of the plight of the native population. After 1945 new tentative approaches, including the introduction of cooperatives and the encouragement of community development, along with the extension and rationalization of social welfare, were implemented in an area previously outside the scope, for all practicable purposes, of provincial governmental services. Beginning in 1957 increased social assistance was provided to the largely indigenous population of the North. Thus, although outlays in the provincial social assistance to the northern areas increased by only $45,000 in the years 1949-57, from $60,000 to $105,000; between the years 1957 and 1963, the increase was in the order of $270,000, from $105,000 to $375,000, still a scandalously small commitment.[33] The extension of services by federal and provincial agencies to Indians and Metis resulted in a greater knowledge of the scandalous conditions in which the native population lived. It was found that a desperate poverty existed in an otherwise expanding economy.

New programs for Indians and Metis thus emerged and very gradually brought the Indian question out of hiding. It is significant that the change was not forced from below, by Indian organizations. Some Indians, to be sure, voiced their opposition to the treatment of the native population. The Indians of coastal British Columbia, in particular, had vigorously (although unsuccessfully) contested the land question at both provincial and federal levels in the 1920s. In the 1940s as well, provincially-based organizations in Alberta, Ontario, Saskatchewan and British Columbia were brought into existence. But these were government-inspired, with little capability and few organizational skills.[34]

The chief impetus for change was generated by developments in the non-Indian community in Canada and abroad. Since 1945 there had been a dramatic change in the relation between white and non-white peoples of the world. The development of an international interest in dependent peoples had a domestic spill-over in Canada. The interest in alleviating the conditions of Indians and improving their socio-economic status in part reflected factors operating on a world scale rather than the result of any specifically Canadian developments.[35]

The Depression and the Second World War permanently altered the Canadian public conception of an appropriate State role with respect to welfare and economic matters. A greater number of governmental services came to be expected as a matter of course, and the administrative capacity of the three levels of Government was expanded to meet these new expectations. Previously, when non-Indian demands on the Government were fairly elementary, there was not a striking divergence (at least in the public mind) between the services that Indians received from the IAB and those that non-Indians received from federal, provincial, and local Governments. With the expansion of services to whites, however, the gap became larger and more conspicuous.[36]

In 1961, the senior administrative officer of the IAB stated that "we have enquiries daily from school children to organizations, and the interest which has been aroused in citizens of non-Indian status particularly in the past five years has been phenomenal."[37] The interest was a prelude to the storm which broke over Canada after 1964. In retrospect the stages in the breakdown of the authority of the IAB seem clear and well-defined: the major revision of the *Indian Act* in 1951; the commissioning and publication of two major socio-economic studies of Indians in British Columbia and Manitoba; the appointment of an Indian, James Gladstone, as a Senator in 1958; the extension of the federal franchise to all Indians in 1960; and the serious attempt to establish a national Indian organization, the National Indian Council. All these appear to be a clear preface to the revolution in Indian affairs. Yet the Governments and the Indians were still groping for future objectives when it became clear after 1964 that major, rather than piecemeal, changes in the social and political status of the Indians and Metis were inevitable. Classically, the *ancien régime* had helped to destroy itself, but no one was prepared for its passing.

From both within and without, the IAB progressively lost whatever legitimacy it had possessed. Obviously it had to be replaced. The question, however, remained: would the strategy of assimilation and reserve segregation be changed? The answer came in the *New Policy*, introduced in July 1969. The whole matter was given a tremendous build-up. The *Hawthorn Report* was seen as the first stage of study on the Indian problem; consultative meetings on the *Indian Act* were held in long sessions between IAB officials and Indians in every province. The *New Policy* ignored both, and it ignored the dismal experience of an attempted termination policy in the U.S.

## The New Policy – The Question of "Special Status"
According to the *New Policy*:

> Indian relations with other Canadians began with special treatment by Government and society, and special treatment has been the rule since Europeans first settled in Canada. Special treatment has made of the Indians a community disadvantaged and apart. . . . To be an Indian must be to be free – free to develop Indian culture in an environment of legal, social and economic equality with other Canadians.[38]

This "special treatment" has had the effect of keeping the Indian people "apart from other Canadians," because, in the words of the *New Policy*: "the Indian people have not been full citizens of the communities and provinces in which they live. They have not been able to enjoy the equality and the benefits which such participation would have offered them." We are reminded that "Canadians, Indians and non-Indians alike, stand at the crossroads." A decisive choice must be made on the issue of permitting the present social and economic gap between Indians and non-Indians to increase, or to permit this growing element of the population a more extensive share in the general well-being.[39]

> For many Indian people one road does exist, the only road that had existed since Confederation and before, a road of different status, blind alley of deprivation and frustration. This road, because it is a separate road, cannot lead to full participation, to equality in practice as well as in theory . . . the treatment resulting from . . . different status has often been worse, sometimes equal and occasionally better than that accorded to their fellow citizens; what matters is that it has been different.[40]

Having concluded that a policy of "special status" results in injustice and deprivation, the *New Policy* sets forth a plan to eliminate all legal and administrative barriers which supposedly deny Indians a right to participate on equal terms with other Canadians. According to its recommendations, the *New Policy* would involve the repeal of the *Indian Act* together with legislative steps which would allow Indians to control their lands and to acquire title to them. Secondly, and concomitantly, the Department of Indian Affairs and Northern Development would see the termination of their Indian affairs functions. In their place the provinces would assume responsibility for Indians just as they have for other citizens in the provinces. To assist the provinces the federal Government would transfer funds normally provided for similar Indian programs. Like other Canadians, therefore, Indians would look to the provinces instead of the federal Government for education, health, welfare and housing services. On the issue of increasing provincial services to the Indians at the expense of the federal role, the Trudeau Government merely issued a *coup de grâce* to a tradition extending back into the 1950s. Certainly by 1969 the provincial Governments had assumed the dominant role in the areas of welfare and education.

Finally, the *New Policy* proposed that the residual responsibilities of the federal Government for programs in the field of Indian affairs would be transferred to other appropriate federal Government departments, such as the Department of Manpower for employment relocation. The *New Policy*, however, indicated that the federal Government would be responsible for providing substantial funds for Indian economic development. According to governmental policy as stated, it was expected that within five years the Indian Affairs Branch would cease to operate.

The *New Policy* is an immensely subtle document. For example, it does not say that policy has been finalized, to be implemented regardless of what Indians or other people say. It does not propose outright elimination or abolition of Indian reserves, nor does it say that the provincial Governments should necessarily take responsibility for Indian lands. Furthermore, it does not propose to disregard the Treaties or to end them unilaterally, and Jean Chretien, Minister of Indian Affairs and Northern Development, has taken great pains to point out that the *New Policy* does not advocate a weakening of Indian culture or identity or, and this is decisive, the assimilation of the Indian people. According to the Minister:

The statement is clear on all these points. On many occasions, both privately and publicly, to Indian and non-Indian people alike, I have tried to clear up these misrepresentations. ... The statement does not propose that the federal Government 'abandon' the Indian people to the provinces without insuring that the provinces have the resources to maintain and improve upon the existing level of programs and services.[41]

The *New Policy*, however, is not what it seems, and goes far beyond subsequent clarifications by Minister Chretien. Its ideology is neatly concealed behind a deluge of clichés about participation and equality. The Indian question is defined as an administrative problem, one that had been discussed ever since Confederation, but most succinctly by the *Machinery of Government Committee* in 1918. According to its report on the selection of an administrative principle for the various Government Departments: "there appear to be only two alternatives, which may be briefly described as distribution according to the persons or classes to be dealt with, and distribution according to the services to be performed."[42] Either the Government has to extend services to Indians as individuals with the same access to these services as other Canadians, or it would have to extend them to a racial group with a distinct identity. In the latter case, the implication would be that the racial group itself would be not only the source but also the substance of the problem. In the former case, the Indian problem would be seen as part of the general low-income problem; a functional principle in this case would lump all poor people together rather than place specific groups under specific ministries for children, paupers, etc.[43]

The *Report* of Diefenbaker's *Joint Parliamentary Committee* attacked the existence of so-called "Lilliputian administrations" in the federal Government:

It is the view, however, of the Joint Committee that the state within the state, that is, the Indian Affairs Branch, must end and that the means to this must be the selection of the alternative principle whereby in each field of Government activity a particular service is rendered to the community as a whole. In this way, Indians and non-Indians become associated together in access to the same Government benefit. Since in education, social welfare and economic development, the provincial Government has the jurisdiction for the non-Indian majority, these same functions should be transferred to the provincial Government for the benefit of Indians also, with the minimum of delay.[44]

One can see, therefore, that there is nothing new in the argument of the *New Policy*. Administrative discontent with the Indian Affairs Branch has had a very long history in Canadian administration. A concept of special status has been repugnant to federal administrators for half a century. Prime Minister Pierre Elliott Trudeau, speaking in Churchill following the publication of the *New Policy*, reminded his listeners that the past had to be forgotten. Yet few government documents have been met with such an outcry from the native population, which is by this time familiar with administrative fiats. The National Indian Brotherhood has condemned it out of hand, and meetings of the various provincial Indian organizations have similarly denounced it as prejudicial to the interests of the indigenous people of Canada.[45]

The reaction of Indians to the *New Policy* was by no means limited to the view much expressed by the major newspapers of the country that "the solution is too abrupt."[46] On this the Indian leadership also agreed. It too noted the waste in human resources from an unemployment rate of 40 to 50 per cent of the adult male Indian population. Beyond the factor of haste, however, the more astute of the Indian leaders realized that the elimination of special status "decisively attacked a whole concept of Indian-White relations in Canada." David Courchene, of the Manitoba Indian Brotherhood, underlined the issue.[47] Essentially, Indian leaders advanced opposing views of the nature of the cleavage between the indigenous population and the larger society. To the Indians, the *New Policy* is clearly assimilationist.[48] The only difference with the past performances of Indian administration is the current emphasis on speed. The policy of reserve segregation and the cautious enfranchisement of acculturated Indians failed; it is now essential to get the Indians off the reserves and force them into an acceptance of white middle class norms. Tactics only have changed; the basic goals are the same. For Jean Chretien, the *New Policy* does indeed provide a framework for Indian aspirations. The absolutely central core of the *New Policy* is the insistence that "the problems of the Indians are similar to those faced by their non-

Indian neighbours.''[49] Indians can and should express their culture in the same way that the Germans, Ukrainians and Jews have retained their cultural heritage in the overall Canadian mosaic.

The proposed policy of termination outlined by the *New Policy* has brought up one of the most difficult issues in Canadian history: defining the type of relationship which exists between the Indians and non-Indians. The federal and provincial Governments have a vision of an essentially harmonious relationship between Indians and non-Indians, a relationship that was regrettably disturbed by the imposition of separate administrative status. Now it is time to deal once and for all with "the anomaly of treaties between groups within society and the Government of that society."[50] For the Indians, on the other hand, a fundamental dialectic of violence divides the indigenous population from the larger society.

Our task is to evaluate the relative merits of these contradictory positions. The problem is best exposed in the form of a question: does "Indianness" place the individual in a ranking qualitatively different from the descendants of European immigrants, even though Indians and Metis from one region to the next in Canada display great differences among themselves?

## An Indian Nation?

Although the preceding sections have emphasized the "colonial" framework of Indian Affairs in Canada, the term has little meaning outside the specific Canadian setting. North American Indians share a broad common experience with indigenous peoples elsewhere, in Africa and Latin America, as well as with the Black population in the United States. But the differences are equally great. To accept parallels from Africa or elsewhere and apply them to Canada without question is absurd. Not only is the historical setting of Canadian Indian and Metis affairs unique, but the available options open to native people in Canada are limited by the Canadian social and political system in which it is embedded. Thus the issues of race and dependence, together with strategies to overcome prevailing disabilities are specific to the Canadian context.

### 1. Race and Colour

The issue of "race" raises difficult questions. Like the Blacks in the United States, the North American Indian fell on the wrong side of a crucial dividing line that separated "acceptable" ethnic groups from "savages" and "slaves." In both cases, the English settlers justified special discriminatory policies and practices directed towards Indians and Blacks which they did not tolerate for the Scots, the French, or even the Irish.[51] In the case of the Negroes in the United States, a self-reinforcing "debasement in slavery and prejudice in the mind" became deeply rooted in American civilization, so that the rationale for racial discrimination was explicitly articulated. In particular, the whole mythology of "colour" was expounded, and linked to the whole nexus of characteristics – living habits, religion, language, facial characteristics – that together implied inferiority. After the abolition of slavery, racial discrimination has remained intact. Indeed, once the vicious cycle of racial hostility has been established; once certain kinds of features are equated with ugliness, low birth and low intelligence; and once the "coloured" race accepts the interpretation thrust upon it by the "whites," it seems almost impossible to break.[52]

North American Indians were treated, in general, with more dignity than the black slaves from Africa, although dignity alone could not save many tribes from liquidation. Aboriginal rights were recognized in English, American and Canadian law; the "treaties" implied the recognition of Indian "nations" while Blacks were dealt with as individuals. One European settler group, the French, managed to get along rather well with the Indians.[53] But land hunger and the need for an internal enemy to display in sharpest colours the virtues and heroism of the new settlers established a fateful link between Indianness, savagery and inferiority. This has been the case in Canada as well as in the United States. In 1871, the Canadian statesman Joseph Howe asserted that British North America had displayed more wisdom and morality in dealing with the Indians than the Americans. It had, he felt, been more just and generous, but also more successful. A hundred years later, Canada must wake up to the fact that racial discrimination is alive and well.[54]

The colour question must be placed in perspective. In the first centuries of contact between Europeans and native people, many writers insisted that Indians were in fact "white," and there were some that romanticized the "noble savage" in smart European drawing-rooms. By the time of the treaties, in fact, there had been a tremendous amount of blood mixing. Some

35

entire bands were fathered by whites themselves. In 1790 a Scotsman by the name of Daniel Sutherland came out in the employ of the Hudson's Bay Company, left it after a short time, and settled down with a Cree wife. She died; he took another; she died, he married yet another. By the three he had twenty-seven children, who in turn had families. In his lifetime, Sutherland had fathered a band, and become Chief.[55]

The treaties made a legal distinction between Indian and Metis; from the point of view of blood content this was an arbitrary division. After the treaties sexual intercourse and inter-marriage between whites and Metis with treaty Indians continued. Today the pure blood Indian exists only in fiction. Rather, there is a broad colour spectrum extending from those Indians who are indistinguishable from whites to those who very definitely bear the features and the colour of the aboriginal population. In many cases it simply is not possible to distinguish Indians or Metis from French Canadians, Ukrainians or other dark skinned Europeans. In California, many Indians are confounded with Mexican Americans.[56] From the point of view of colour the North American Indian has a far greater opportunity to assimilate than other racial minorities.

Intermarriages with Indians who "look Indian" are very uncommon – much less so than in the immediate pre-colonialization phase. But sexual contact is frequent between the lowest levels of white and Indian society, producing large numbers of illegitimate children with the most broad array of skin colour and features. The United States military base across the border to the South has added yet another variant to "Indian" features in the Prairie region in Canada – the indigenous mulatto (a rather pleasing mixture, in fact).

Before the collapse of the river and hunting economies the Indian and Metis on the frontier never considered themselves as humble hangers-on to white civilization. Louis Riel, for example, may have acknowledged the "humble origin" of his "race" but he was also proud of his Indian ancestry. He emphasized that the Metis honoured their Indian mothers as much as their white fathers. His sense of independence was manifested in the two Rebellions in the Northwest Territories in which he figured so prominently.[57] In her excellent work on Western Canada, Irene Spry similarly refers to the *élan* of the Metis as long as their way of life was not undermined.[58]

36

In the final analysis, however, the stereotype of the mentally soft and shiftless Indian triumphed, and the dominant white society in Canada displays a great sensitivity toward the colour factor which identifies "Indianness." This is clear in the general ignorance of variations among Indians and Metis across the country. The majority look "Indian" and are defined and treated by whites, of whatever nationality, simply as "Indians."

In short, the "race" factor shows no signs of disappearing in white-Indian relations in Canada. Indian children must always come to terms with their features and colour; their parents must help them cope with the association of "badness" and native features which they sense in the larger society. In Indian families of mixed parentage those children who look white play with white students of the same age; those who retain Indian features tend to have their range of friends restricted to Indians, especially in the post-grade school age. Although the Indians and Metis in Canada do not as yet indulge in skin powders or bleach their hair, the colour factor must not be neglected in a study of "race relations" in Canada.

## 2. Dependence

Although they have not clearly elaborated their position, most Indian and Metis leaders in the past decade have increasingly resisted the suggestion that Indians are, or will eventually be, assimilated into the larger society in Canada. Their point is that a solution is not to be found in merely a more just distribution of goods and services; participation must also include the choice of "meaningful alternatives." By this they mean the recognition by white society that Canada includes not just two nations – the French and the English – but also a third main cultural stem – the indigenous population – that by virtue of its heritage and history has a special claim to be respected and encouraged.

Indians therefore want more than to be allowed in; they want the entire country to recognize the uniqueness of their contribution to the rich and colourful heritage of Canada. They have defined this goal as *integration*, as distinguished from assimilation. Integration as a policy was already advocated in 1891 by a short-lived periodical called the *Canadian Indian*:

> Would it not be pleasanter and ever safer, to us, to have living in our midst a contented, well-to-do, self-respecting,

thriving community of Indians, rather than a set of dependent, dissatisfied, half-educated and half-anglicized paupers?[59]

Interestingly enough, it is possible to find virtual endorsements of integration as a policy made by officials during the tumultuous years of Indian affairs after the breakdown of the policy of reserve segregation:

> Progress will be made in direct ratio to the degree in which the public and governments realize that the participation of the Indians in the social and economic life of Canada on a basis of equality of opportunity need not, in fact must not, be contingent on the Indians' surrendering their culture, their reserves and the special rights that have been conferred upon them as the first citizens of Canada, unless the Indians so desire.[60]

The suggestion would be, in comments of this kind, that specific Indian norms be accepted at face value; that the indigenous population be recognized as standing apart from the larger society. The publication of the *New Policy* in July of 1969 ended the official talk of integration in this sense once and for all.

The dilemma of integration is not specific to Canada. It haunts all colonial situations where a dominant white society has established itself over a weaker indigenous population that is now demanding social and ethnic equality. In Canada, the dilemma may be especially severe because of the society's particularly conscientious attention to values stressing liberalism, individualism, and the necessity of free choice. Few societies are as exposed to severe contradictions in their basic value systems as is the Canadian, simply because it is, in general, relatively humane and gentle. Unfortunately, the demand by the native people for integration confronts Canadians with a unique problem. The claim of the French Canadians for linguistic and cultural rights is set down in the *British North America Act*, and the vast majority of the French live in a province which enjoys sovereignty in many important ways. Quebec also can, and may, declare itself an independent state to ensure the survival of its culture. An institutional framework exists within which the special national demands of French Canadians can be recognized. The French Canadians share a common culture with other European Canadians; the Indians and Metis, on the other hand, form a far more distinct "national group."

Given their technical inadequacies and the scattering of reserves and communities, however, there is not the remotest chance of the native people forming a viable economy or escaping almost total dependence on the white-controlled economy. The achievement of levels of economic and social development comparable to those of the white population would require such a heavy dependence on external aid and such intense participation in the economy as to rule out any significant degree of economic independence.[61]

An insight into the extreme level of dependence of the Indians can be easily gained by examining conventional indicators of socio-economic development. According to the Saskatchewan Provincial Task Force on Education:

A total of 10,010 Treaty Indian students were in schools in Saskatchewan in February [1969] ... the most revealing aspect of the enrolment figures is the sharp and continuous decrease in enrolment beginning as early as grade 3 and continuing on with increasing speed until, with Indian students, only .5% are in grade 12 and in northern Saskatchewan only .3%.... Several conclusions can be reached about this sad situation. First, the students are inadequately prepared to continue on in an academic stream. Second, parents are not encouraging their children to go through school, and the pupils see little point in continuing school for various reasons.[62]

The following table gives a further indication of the extremely disadvantaged condition of the Indians in the educational system of the province.

Employment and income statistics provide even more telling evidence of Indian deprivation. In Saskatchewan in 1969, of a total employable reserve population of 11,634, only 698, or 6.2%, had full-time jobs. More than twice this number held some sort of part-time employment, but the income from this employment is not high, given the extreme marginality of traditional part-time occupations such as hunting and fishing. The level of earned income decisively undercuts any notion of Indian reserve prosperity. Out of the Saskatchewan reserve population of 26,000, only 6,000 had a cash income in 1969. 60.7% of these earned less than $1,000; 21.3% between $1,000 and $1,999; 6.6% between $2,000 and $2,999; 5.3% between $3,000 and $3,999; and 6.1% over $4,000.[63]

**Table 2**
**School Enrolment by Grades as of September 1971**
**in Federal and Provincial Schools in Saskatchewan**

|       | Federal | Provincial | Totals |
|-------|---------|------------|--------|
| K1    | 254     | —          | 254    |
| K2    | 598     | 327        | 925    |
| 1     | 548     | 1,197      | 1,745  |
| 2     | 398     | 960        | 1,358  |
| 3     | 382     | 803        | 1,185  |
| 4     | 339     | 789        | 1,128  |
| 5     | 272     | 745        | 1,017  |
| 6     | 259     | 677        | 936    |
| 7     | 143     | 665        | 808    |
| 8     | 104     | 479        | 583    |
| 9     | 46      | 393        | 439    |
| 10    | —       | 262        | 262    |
| 11    | —       | 156        | 156    |
| 12    | —       | 87         | 87     |
| Spec. | 15      | 294        | 309    |
| Totals | 3,358  | 7,834      | 11,192 |

*Source: Census File Cards for October 1971, and Age-Grade-Sex Reports for September 1971.*

A number of reserves in Canada have much higher incomes. According to the *Hawthorn Report*, seven Indian bands of the 36 studied across Canada had a real income per capita of more than $500 annually.[64] There is no question but that there is considerable variation from band to band, from the highly developed Skidegate and Caughnawaga to the extremely deprived Plains Cree. But let us be clear on one point: a situation in which the Indian population as a whole has an average income of $300 is lamentable.

Some observers have claimed that the Indians might emulate Hutterites or other groups who have managed to retain a relatively diversified and self-contained culture, religion, language, and dress in the larger society.[65] However, all the factors which account for the viability of groups like the Hutterites are absent in the Indian case. They do not have entrenched habits of work and thrift; or a highly centralized and authoritarian system of internal government to guarantee the enforcement of norms and habits which ensure community survival. The Indian reserves and the Metis communities can not either singly or together form viable independent units. The very most that even the highly developed reserves and communities can aim for is municipal status and local self-government. As a result the Indians and the Metis do not espouse a separatist ideology. There is no talk of demanding a separate state; there is full awareness of the dependence of the Indian and Metis on the larger society. Nevertheless, there has been a marked increase in Pan-Indian consciousness in the last decade.

## Conclusion: The Moral Vacuum

Not a few Indians and Metis have found mental peace when they have read:

> The colonial world is a world cut in two ... the zone where the native lives is not complementary to the zone inhabited by the settlers. The two zones are opposed but not in the service of a higher unity ... the settler and the native are old acquaintances. ... It is the settler who has brought the native into existence, and who perpetuates his existence. The settler owes the fact of his existence, that is to say his property, to the colonial system.[66]

The applicability of Frantz Fanon's stark imagery to the "Mississippi of the North"[67] stems from his premise of conflict rather than harmony between the native and white populations. The two in Canada have lived together not because they shared a consensus of values but because there was no alternative for the natives. The weakness of the Fanon argument, on the other hand, derives from its lack of immediate relevance for practicable programs. Not even the most radical native leaders exhort the Indians to kill the surrounding farmers or to indulge in violence for the sake of psychological revival. The dependency of the native population on the larger society is so intense that there is no conceivable chance of full liberation. It is condemned to an existence in white society forever. A cruel future. As in the United States, the problem of race in Canada is not just a matter of legal and political equality. Indians are born with the most profound disability that Canadian society can impose upon a citizen. They are poor because they are Indian; and Indian because they are poor.

The settler society robbed the Indians of their land, and

locked them up on reserves. But it did something even worse, it destroyed the Indian religions and the morale of the Indian-Metis population. Now, when the political fetters on the Indians are loosening, the moral vacuum is almost complete. Pan-Indianism is merely a common awareness; it is not a rallying cry. Yet without an ideology of revival the task of rebuilding the Indian community in Canada will be insurmountable. The Black experience in the United States is instructive; religion has been a formidable instrument in overcoming the disunity in the Black community.

Some Indians comfort themselves with the ideological superiority of the Indian culture and the belief that their example will affect the larger society in North America.[68] While it is true that the revival of Indian consciousness forms part of a widespread questioning of North American liberal society, while it is inseparable from student rebellion and the alienation of the youth and the Blacks in America, there is little evidence of an ideological spread from the Indians to the larger society. More importantly, there is as yet no evidence that this new ideology has resulted in creative programs for either the reserves or the cities.

Once the overall situation resulting from colonial heritage has been accepted and defined, the question of choosing a strategy remains. White society controls the resources of the country. It is therefore incumbent upon it to initiate and implement policies that match the urgency of the problem. In the field of urbanization, it is particularly urgent that Governments and pressure groups respond with concepts that transcend the settler experience and that experiment with new structures.

---

[1] Irene Spry. "The Transition from a Nomadic to a Settled Economy in Western Canada 1865-1896," *Transactions of the Royal Society in Canada*, Vol. 6, Series 4, June, 1968.

[2] Canada, *The Canadian Indian*, Department of Indian Affairs and Northern Development, Indian Affairs Branch, Ottawa, Queen's Printer, 1966.

[3] *Hawthorn Report*, p. 368.

[4] Allan C. Harper, "Canada's Indian Administration: Basic Concepts and Objectives," *America Indigena*. Vol. V, 1945, p. 130.

[5] Canada, *Sessional Papers* (House of Commons), 1895. (*North West Mounted Police*, Appendix A.) See also *Sessional Papers*, 1894: "A few Indians came into the district with passes from the reserves but gave no trouble" (*North West Mounted Police*, Regina, Northwest Territories, 15 December, 1894, Appendix C, p. 63).

The reports of the North West Mounted Police make many references to the Metis as go-betweens in the liquor racket in particular. The evidence from Marcel Giraud, *op. cit.*, however, makes it clear that the Metis were considered of the same racial group as the Indians. Irene Spry puts much stress on the division of the Metis after 1885 into that group which refused to adjust and whose position became even worse than that of the Indians, and that which chose to adapt to the new civilization of the whites and was able to assimilate into the white society. (Spry, *op. cit.*, p. 196). The North West Mounted Police found the liquor business to be particularly problematical because the Metis were not legal wards of the State. The Metis did not act as go-betweens after the turn of the century. The Indian and white cultures after the end of the primitive fur, buffalo, and river economy became increasingly polarized.

6 Department of Citizenship and Immigration, Indian Affairs Branch, *The Indian in Transition, op. cit.*, p. 10.

7 Alexis de Tocqueville, *Democracy in America*, Max Lerner and L. P. Mayer, eds., New York, Harper, 1965, Vol. I, p. 312.

8 The *Indian Act* gives the federal government extraordinary powers over Indian lands. For example, Section 18 (1): "Subject to this Act, reserves are held by Her Majesty for the use and benefit of the respective bands for which they have been set apart; and subject to this Act and to terms of any treaty or surrender, the Governor in Council may determine whether any purpose for which lands in a reserve are used or are to be used is for the use and benefit of the band." For recent discussions of legal status of Indians in Canada see generally, *Native Rights in Canada*, second edition, edited by Peter A. Cumming and Neil Mickenberg, Indian Eskimo Association of Canada, Toronto, 1972.

9 Louis Hartz, "Violence and Legality in Fragment Cultures," *The Canadian Historical Review*, June, 1969, pp. 134ff.

10 Department of Citizenship and Immigration, Indian Affairs Branch, *Treaty Six*, Ottawa, 1961, p. 10.

11 Canada, *Sessional Papers* (House of Commons), 1895, Appendix A, pp. 247-248.

12 Ruth Matheson Buck, "The Story of the Ahenakews," *Saskatchewan History*, Vol. 17, No. 1, 1964, p. 7.

13 *Hawthorn Report*, Vol. 1, p. 365.

14 *Report of the Indian Branch of the Department of the Secretary of State for the Provinces*, Ottawa, 1870, p. 4, as quoted in *Ibid.*, p. 127.

15 D. C. Scott, "The Future of the Indians," *Canada and Its Provinces*, Vol. 8, pp. 622-623, as quoted in Harper, *op. cit.*, p. 127.

16 Department of Citizenship and Immigration, Indian Affairs Branch, *The Indian in Transition*, Ottawa, 1961, p. 10.

17 *Ibid.*, pp. 123-124.

18 Canada, *Sessional Papers*, (House of Commons) 1881. *The Report of the Department of Indian Affairs*, 1881, p. 8.

19 Marcel Giraud, *op. cit.*, p. 2. (Giraud's work is the only good material available on the Metis of Canada.) The term "half-breed head of family" referred to all persons married by July 15, 1870. The term "Metis child" applied without distinction of age to all persons not married by that date (N. O. Cote, Department of the Interior, Ottawa, April 14, 1899).

[20] The spoliation here took place on a broader scale and with more cynicism than in Manitoba, and under conditions identical with those characterizing the fraudulent dispossessions of the southern African Metis group of Rehoboth Basters, who were likewise a primitive group, and likewise ready to alienate, for small sums of money or for objects without value, the rich lands which had been set aside for them by the German Government. . . . In the last analysis, the whole operation benefited only a minority who made intelligent use of the capital assured by the negotiation of scrips in order to increase their livestock and agricultural equipment. Instead, the operation was a principal factor in creating a class of rich speculators, "half-breed scrip millionaires," whose fortunes were victims of their own ignorance, their weakness and their ill-adaptation to the new economy. *Ibid.*, pp. 4-5.

[21] *Ibid.*, p. 11.

[22] Canada, *Sessional Papers*, (House of Commons), 1891, pp. 153-154.

[23] *Hawthorn Report*, Vol. 1, p. 265ff.

[24] Note that the Metis were not within the special structure of Indian Affairs, and yet suffered much the same fate.

[25] Only individuals with the legal status of Indians can belong to an Indian band. "A band consists of all those people who, on May 26, 1874, were legitimate members of a band for whom land had been set aside; all male descendents in the male line of male persons thus qualifying; the legitimate children of such persons; the illegitimate children of qualifying females, provided that the Registrar of the Department has not declared that the father of the child was not an Indian; and the wife or widow of a qualifying person." (Quoted in *Hawthorn Report*, Vol. 1, p. 271.)

[26] *Hawthorn Report*, cited above.

[27] Department of Indian Affairs and Northern Development, The Honourable Jean Chretien, Minister, *The New Indian Policy*, Ottawa, July, 1969. The "policy of termination" outlines the necessity for the abolition of "special status" for the registered Indians of Canada. It will be dealt with shortly in this chapter.

[28] Department of Indian Affairs and Northern Development, Indian Affairs Branch, Departmental Statistics Division, *Survey of Indian Bands and Reserves*, Ottawa, January, 1971, Table 7.

[29] The Honourable Ellen L. Fairclough, "Indian Affairs in 1960," *Monetary Times Annual*, 1961, p. 37 and "Indian Affairs in 1961," *Monetary Times Annual*, 1962, pp. 36-47.

[30] Canada, *Report of the Joint Parliamentary Committee on Indian Affairs*, Ottawa, 1961.

[31] Department of Indian Affairs and Northern Development, Indian Affairs Branch, Departmental Statistics Division, *Survey of Indian Bands and Reserves*, Ottawa, January, 1971, Tables 3 and 4.

[32] The Honourable Ellen L. Fairclough, "Indian Affairs in 1959," *Monetary Times Annual*, 1960, p. 38.

[33] H. Buckley, et. al., "The Indians and Metis of Northern Saskatchewan: A Report on Economic and Social Development," Centre for Community Studies, University of Saskatchewan, Saskatoon, 1963, p. 24, fig. 6.

[34] E. Palmer Patterson II, *The Canadian Indian: A History Since 1500*, Toronto, Collier-Macmillan Canada Limited, 1972, pp. 170-171.

[35] *Hawthorn Report*, Vol. 1, p. 362.

[36] *Ibid.*, pp. 362-363.

[37] *Report of the Joint Parliamentary Committee*, p. 343.

[38] Department of Indian Affairs and Northern Development, *The New Indian Policy*, Ottawa, July, 1969.

[39] *Ibid.*

[40] *Ibid.*

[41] *The Indian News*, November, 1969, p. 4.

[42] As quoted in John Melling, "Indian Affairs in Canada," *Continuous Learning*, Vol. I, 1962, p. 73.

[43] *Ibid.*, p. 74, and Vladimir Salyzyn, "Goals in Indian Affairs," *Canadian Welfare*, Vol. 42, No. 2, pp. 79-81.

[44] Melling, *op. cit.*, p. 73.

[45] *The Indian News*, October, 1969, pp. 1-3.

[46] *Toronto Globe and Mail*, July 1, 1969.

[47] "Indians today are organizing, are learning to speak for themselves, are identifying for the first time goals and objectives, developing new aspirations, and creating new relationships compatible with our desires for independence.... It seems that the Government, being aware of the increasing strength and ability of Indian organizations, has decided to move now before they become too difficult to deal with or are able to effectively defend themselves. In Manitoba, we have recently embarked upon a new 'partnership concept.'... This whole program is now threatened ... we are bargained over in the federal-provincial negotiations like cattle in an auction mart." *Omphalos*, July 23-29, 1969.

[48] Indeed, it appears so to the general white public – which has endorsed the *New Policy*. The reaction of a Salvation Army attendant in Saskatoon to the announcement of the *New Policy* was typical: "It is high time the Indians were kicked off the reserves and learned to sink or swim. A few might make it. They have had handouts long enough and it is time that they learned to shift for themselves."

[49] *The New Policy*, p. 10.

[50] *Ibid.*, p. 11.

[51] Winthrop D. Jordon, *White Over Black*, Baltimore, Penguin Books, 1969, pp. 85-98.

[52] *Ibid.*, pp. 482-486; 583.

[53] *Native Rights in Canada, op. cit.*, pp. 65-68.

[54] *Ibid.*, p. 73.

[55] David G. Mandelbaum, "Anthropology and People: The World of the Plains Cree," *University Lectures*, University Lecture Series, No. 12, p. 7.

[56] John A. Price, "Migration and Adaptation of American Indians to Los Angeles," *Human Organization*, Vol. 27, No. 2, (Summer, 1968), p. 173.

[57] George F. Stanley, *The Birth of Western Canada*, Toronto, University of Toronto Press, 1961, pp. 6-12.

[58] Spry, *op. cit.*, pp. 193-194.

[59] As quoted in Harper, *op. cit.*, p. 129.

[60] Department of Citizenship and Immigration, Indian Affairs Branch, *Administration of Indian Affairs*, Ottawa, 1964, p. 4.

[61] *Hawthorn Report*, p. 23.

[63] Department of Indian Affairs and Northern Development, Indian Affairs Branch, Departmental Statistics Division, *Survey of Indian Bands and Reserves*, Tables 24 and 25.

[64] *Hawthorn Report*, pp. 95-96.

[65] *Hawthorn Report*, Vol. 1, pp. 188ff.

[66] Frantz Fanon, *The Wretched of the Earth*, New York, Evergreen, 1965, pp. 39-40.

[67] Howard Adams, *Interview*, August 5, 1969.

[68] Vine Deloria, as quoted in Stan Steiner, *The New Indians*, New York, Macmillan, 1969, pp. 9-10.

"It isn't that there are only 500,000 of us Indians . . . what is important is that we have a superior way of life, we Indians have more human philosophy of life. We Indians will show the country how to act human. Someday, this country will revise its Constitution, its laws, in terms of human beings instead of property. If red power is to be power of this country, it is because it is ideological."

# 2

## The Native Aristocracy
## in the City

The treatment afforded the Canadian Indians and Metis excluded them from a creative role in the society and economy of the country. Indian businessmen, professionals, and white-collar workers formed a minute percentage of the native population before 1960, and the social and political mechanisms maintaining dependence remained intact. The undermining of these controls coincided with large-scale migration to urban areas in the last decade. Dislocation, unemployment, and poverty are some of the consequences usually associated with migration under these circumstances.

But one segment of the native population in Canadian cities has fared surprisingly well. The number of families that have successfully adapted to city life in Saskatoon, Saskatchewan is small (about twenty-five), but they form an important group that must not be overlooked in a study of urban Indian social structure. Its ranks include a Metis university professor, a successful self-employed Metis business man, a not-overly successful self-employed Indian, a semi-skilled worker, two unskilled labourers, and the remainder who are employees of federal and provincial agencies and organizations dealing with welfare and Indian affairs.

Relative to other Indians and Metis in the city, the group forms something of an aristocracy. The members of this group have been designated the *Affluent* native people. Although potentially misleading, the designation *Affluent* appears the most appropriate for this category. These families are definitely not wealthy, but are very well off when compared to other members of the indigenous population in the city. Moreover, in the relations with Indians and Metis in the city their "affluence" is a decisive factor in defining their superior status. The extent of their adaptation to the urban environment can be seen by measuring their observed behaviour against conventional indicators of social and personal adjustment.

## 1. Job Stability

One of the most striking characteristics of the *Affluent* Indians and Metis is steady employment, with the resultant absence of dependence on public welfare. With only two exceptions, all the *Affluent* Indians and Metis earned less than $10,000 a year in 1969. Nonetheless, the earnings were sufficient to allow these families a fairly comfortable existence, and the stability of their jobs frees them from the anxiety of frequent lay-offs. In many cases, the Indians who are employed as labourers work many hours overtime in order to supplement regular earnings.

If one can speak of an employment structure in a group so small, the most interesting feature is the large number employed by Government or Government-financed agencies and organizations. Increasingly in Saskatoon the remaining members of this group who are labourers find their way into Government bureaucracies or Government-financed native organizations. The change is considered a promotion; the *Affluent* are upwardly mobile but within the world of Indian affairs.

## 2. Housing

The *Affluent* Indians and Metis in the city live in comfortable private homes in the rather better white neighbourhoods. They are by no means lavish suburban dwellings, but compare favourably with those of the lower middle class – frame one-storey bungalows with private gardens in the $15,000-$20,000 range, purchased on long-term homeowners' mortgages. The location of the home puts them in good school districts as well. The *Affluent* Indians live well away from the older and shadier parts of town in the most recent subdivisions.

## 3. Intra-City Mobility

In striking contrast to other Indians and Metis in the city, the *Affluent* do not rapidly change addresses within the city. The movement to the city is carefully planned and phased to insure that adequate housing at a permanent address is obtained. If some time is necessary in order to complete arrangements for the purchase of a new house, stable interim accommodation is arranged. Whereas it is literally impossible to keep track of most Indians and Metis when they arrive in town, the *Affluent* immediately install telephones, bring in heavy furniture, and in general set up shop as if they were there to stay.

The pattern of migration among the *Affluent* is not typical of the other immigrant populations that settled in Saskatoon. The Ukrainians, for example, when they arrived in large numbers at the turn of the century, almost immediately established an ethnic enclave in the poor areas of the West Side. Here the first generation developed a network of community institutions, grouped largely around their Churches, to buttress the struggle for financial security. Their children properly schooled and acculturated, moved out of the West Side and into the more prosperous residential districts.[1] By the second generation Ukrainian cultural patterns had almost completely eroded. The third generation shows no loyalty whatsoever toward the original West Side Ghetto that had so greatly benefited their relatives.

The *Affluent* Indians, however, move immediately to the better neighbourhoods without an initial period in an ethnic enclave. From the vantage-point of the reserve, they recognize, and claim access to, the urban facilities that denote middle class respectability. Their perceptions of power relationships within the city are very sophisticated, and their expectations are high. The *Affluent* have no desire to emulate the patient, plodding and sacrificing first-generation Slavs.

## 4. Family Stability

The movement to the city of the *Affluent* does not eliminate extended family relationships. Generally speaking, the extended family is characterized by: joint residence of two or more related nuclear family units; the existence of joint family activities by the extended family members as an organized unit (ranging from economic and legal to welfare and leisure); assistance among individual relatives, in the form of gifts or services; and the existence of friendship networks joining kinsmen. Not long ago, it was assumed that urbanization cut the links between an individual family and the larger kinship group. Given the complexity of city life and the loss of dependence on particular persons, so the argument went, the nuclear family increasingly lost contact

49

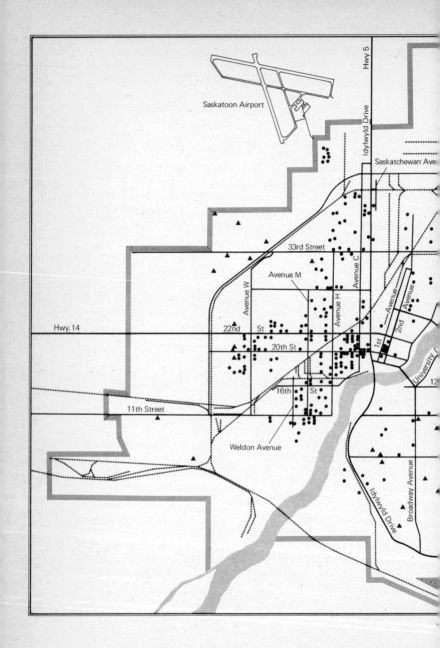

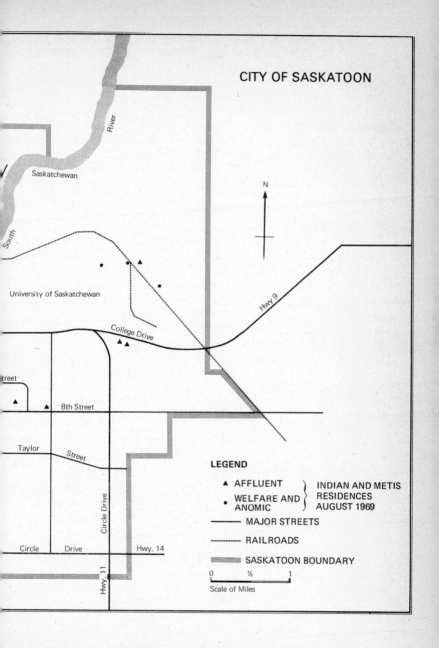

CITY OF SASKATOON

N

River

Saskatchewan

South

University of Saskatchewan

Hwy 9

College Drive

treet

8th Street

Taylor Street

Circle Drive

Circle Drive Hwy. 14

Hwy. 11

LEGEND

▲ AFFLUENT        } INDIAN AND METIS
● WELFARE AND     RESIDENCES
   ANOMIC            AUGUST 1969

——— MAJOR STREETS

·········· RAILROADS

▬▬▬ SASKATOON BOUNDARY

0      ½      1

Scale of Miles

with relatives. Family life, so to speak, was stripped to its bare essentials. In most homes of the *Affluent* Indians however, one finds siblings or parents or cousins from the reserve, or relatives in town. It is by no means unusual to come across a household where the nuclear family of the husband, wife and children has been joined by grandparents, daughters-in-law, brothers-in-law and their children. In some respects it is similar to urban migration in Latin America or Africa, where tenacious extended family relationships are maintained in the burgeoning cities.[2]

Nevertheless, in every case family life is stable. None of the units involved are based on common-law relationships; in each, both the father and mother are present at home. Barring the ups and downs of marital life, the family stability of the *Affluent* Indians and Metis in the city is altogether comparable to that of the white middle class with whom they live. The families are careful to curtail those aspects of extended family life that inhibit the stability and achievement of the immediate family. In every case emphasis is given to the survival of the nuclear family, with extended family patterns occupying a secondary role.

From the earliest contacts with the indigenous population, Church and Government administrators attempted to break tribal-family patterns, and to inculcate the norms of the nuclear family in the life-style of Indians and Metis. The reserves were, among other things, administrative units where tribal, family and moral practices could be abolished by the discreet use of economic and religious incentives. A. J. Markle, Agent of the Blackfoot Reserve in Alberta, described his reaction to polygamy among the Indians:

It may be remembered that, in my last report, I expressed thankfulness that there had been no plural marriages during the preceding year. That report was barely out of my hand when I learned that three members of the band were dissatisfied with one wife each and had taken another. I immediately directed that the rations of these families be withheld until such time as they saw fit to obey the rules in this respect. One family missed one ration, and then decided that it was better to abide by the rules. The other two families held out for several rations, and then they succumbed and put away wife No. 2. The rationing of able-bodied men and women had many objectionable features to me, but I must confess

52

that, in these three instances, it gave a leverage to settle an objectionable custom, for the time being at least.[3]

At the level of the *Affluent* there is reason to believe that the strategy was relatively successful: there appears to be little inherent tension between the demands of the extended family and the necessities of nuclear family behaviour. At certain times a decision must be made to limit the number of relatives in the house, but this is done relatively simply *without endangering the fabric of the nuclear family itself.*

## 5. Visibility

One of the terms most frequently used to describe the Indian and Metis sub-culture in Canadian cities is "hidden." It refers to the growth of Indian slums, of a population that is poor, transient, broken and hiding from the rest of the city. "Hidden" implies social, economic and political maladjustment; it purports to describe a minority that is too frightened to emerge from its bleak surroundings and which inhabits parts of the city that the white middle class never sees.[4]

It is clear that the *Affluent* Indians and Metis share none of these characteristics. They do not live hidden away from the white middle class; instead, their houses are embedded in good white neighbourhoods. Their jobs, especially those in the bureaucracies, place them in day-to-day contact with whites of some standing and education in the larger community.

Moreover, the *Affluent* are constantly in the news, heading up some new organization or acting as "spokesmen" or "leaders" before diverse conferences dealing with poverty or the plight of the indigenous population. Native participants at conferences and panel discussions are always chosen from this group. Thus they interact very often with white community leaders; they have access to the mass media; and several have become well known in the areas surrounding Saskatoon as well as in the city itself.

Finally, the *Affluent* are not hard to find. They are anxious to place themselves on display to white interviewers and students of Indian and Metis affairs and the Indian Affairs Branch enjoys pointing them out to visitors as local success stories. One white Indian Affairs Branch official rather gracelessly remarked that "they are altogether different from the Indians." It would appear that the *Affluent* have been accustomed to positions of leadership; they are able to relate very effectively with white institutions and community leaders.

## 6. Personal Disintegration

It is widely accepted that Indians and Metis in the city have suffered a high level of personal disorganization. The term would include the various combinations of attitudes, behaviour patterns, and limitations of character and personality that prevent the individual and the group from effectively adjusting to, and participating successfully in, the larger society. Economic deterioration and dependency are thus accompanied by drunkenness, sexual promiscuity, laziness, irresponsibility, neglect of the family, etc. Difficult as these factors are to measure, according to many authors, the North American Indians exhibit signs of breakdown.

Indians and Metis in Saskatchewan, unquestionably account for a disproportionate number of the poor, dependent and unemployed. According to the *Hawthorn Report*, 86.5 per cent of the households on the Piapot Reserve were receiving welfare.[5] According to one authoritative study, 35 per cent of the inmates of jails and training schools are of Indian ancestry, although they make up less than 4 per cent of the population.[6] The illegitimacy rates on most reserves are considerably higher than those in the larger society.[7]

Among the *Affluent* Indians however, there appears to be little evidence of personal disorganization. They are employed; drunkenness does not seem to be a problem; there have been no reported cases of attempted suicide or of petty crime. The odd case of illegitimacy resembles that in white middle class families whose children commit the occasional indiscretion. In general, a high level of personal discipline is exhibited, even ostentatiously. Many feel compelled to castigate other Indians and Metis for their bad habits and loose living, with the implicit claim that they have overcome such problems. Rarely have the families gone so far as to reject liquor altogether, but it is clear that such items are purchased only as the family budget permits.

## 7. Identity in the City

One of the most interesting conclusions of the *Hawthorn Report* concerned the relationship between personal disorganization and the degree of contact with white society. It stated that "the communities which appear to have the highest incidence of personal disorganization are those in which there is access to white communities and considerable interaction at certain levels with whites."

The *Affluent* Indians and Metis in the cities, however, do not appear to suffer from their close contact with white society. There is little evidence among this group of an identity crisis. Each family spoke with some emotion about the reserve, but each was content in the city and expressed satisfaction at the decision to move there. They were not lonesome; they were not disoriented. The *Affluent* Indians and Metis are the self-conscious elite of the native minority in the city.

The *Affluent*, however, do not associate intimately with whites. Despite daily contact with white colleagues in the bureaucracies, or in other jobs, Indians in this group rarely establish close personal relationships with them. Instead, the primary group remains limited to the immediate families and other Indians in their class. The urban "community" for the *Affluent* remains very small, characterized by a small array of Indian institutions and organizations supporting this native group.

Increasingly, the *Affluent* appear to share a common consciousness of Indianness. "Pan-Indianism," as this phenomenon is now labelled, has unquestionably matured in the *Affluent* community in Saskatoon in the last years. One indication is the wholesale collapse of Christianity among these Indians and Metis, even the Indian Churchmen in the group – once the pride of Indian affairs and the missionaries. Not a single family or individual in the city displayed even a lingering loyalty to the most pervasive ideological movement on the reserve; many now speak with great interest about indigenous religious and cultural practices. Many have also renewed their interest in Indian languages and native art work.

Occasionally, Pan-Indianism is reinforced by a massive incident of discrimination which reminds them that they are not quite full members of the larger society. Thus one *Affluent* Indian family, with an impeccable credit rating and the support of the Indian Affairs Branch for the purchase of a new home, discovered that the bank in question did not deal with Indians, no matter what their background and qualifications. The husband was not only a member of one of the leading Indian families of Saskatchewan, but also a veteran and an extremely well-paid mechanic. Nonetheless, after initial approval by the

Saskatoon branch of the bank, the head office flatly refused to renegotiate a mortgage.

But Pan-Indianism among the *Affluent* appears to be more than a reaction to discrimination. It is an expression of a common heritage and a common conflict with the alien society that engulfed them. They claim to be members of a distinct nation within Canada not only because of a lamentable history of despoliation, but also because of the unique history of the indigenous population in Canada from the beginning. Whatever it amounts to in practice, the *Affluent* are leading a revival of Indian consciousness. Even for the most privileged Indians and Metis in the city, the social and psychological awareness of Indian identity is ever present.

## The "Leading Families" on the Reserves

The *Affluent* native people have accomplished in a few years what it took leaders of other ethnic groups, in some cases, much longer to achieve. They have secure incomes, positions of leadership, and give every evidence of having mastered the multiple crises of adjustment normally associated with urbanization. They display, in short, a firm commitment to the major institutions in the city, and are well beyond the poverty line.

Which Indians are successful in the city? Indian and Metis rural communities are assumed to be poverty-stricken. Since the native minority in the city is very new, first-generation, it is far from clear why some Indians and Metis have adapted while others have not. But older Indians do not hesitate in replying to this question: "The ones who made out well on the reserve."

In fact, an analysis of Indian migration from individual reserves unequivocally supports this position. Those individuals and families who were successful on the reserve appear to have had remarkably little difficulty in making the transition to urban life. Indeed, the ease of the transition has been extraordinary, a little too good. If the *Affluent* have had such few difficulties, while the vast majority live on skid row, they must have migrated from the reserves under very unusual circumstances. What happened on the reserves to condition a few families to success, and the majority to failure, when they venture into the city?

The contention here is that Indian administration since the establishment of the reserves has permitted a small elite of nuclear families to thrive, while allowing the vast majority to sink into a miserable dependent existence based on extended kinship relationships. A deep wedge therefore was driven between the leading families and the majority of Indians within reserve boundaries. There were other divisions as well, but the most profound was the cleavage between "leaders" who allied themselves with the Indian administration, and their less fortunate followers.

One example from the Swallow Lake Reserve in northern Saskatchewan illustrates the role of Indian affairs in distorting family relationships through favoured treatment to recognized leaders. In the 1930s a decision was made by Jack Thomas, the farm instructor, to purchase more draught horses for the reserve farmers. The money itself came from the band fund, accumulated from the sale of a portion of the reserve in 1903, and from the sale of Ten Islands Reserve two years earlier. (Since a number of band families had joined the Swallow Lake Reserve, the band obtained a portion of the proceeds.) It was therefore a purchase for the collectivity, the band fund being held in trust by the IAB.

When the animals arrived, few Indians knew how to care for them. By this time the only two leading farmers were Thomas McKnight and his hired man, Samuel Neville. The other farming families were long since gone, following the great decline of reserve property after 1905. The result was that many horses were not properly tended. Jack Thomas therefore gave them to Thomas McKnight, causing an uproar in the band. The decision, however, was not reversed. Thus the *band* fund was used to benefit *two families* that were united by marriage and already economically separated from the other families. The intervention, made with the objective of fostering "leading families," obviously drove a wedge between Thomas McKnight and the band. To maintain this new source of power, he had to retain the favour of the Agent. The redirection of band funds into private hands subtly redefined power relationships on the reserves, isolating the "leading families" on the one hand, and redefining their relations with the white world – the farm instructor and the Agent on the other. They were favoured families, but at the price of hostility and separation from the band.

In fact, the social stratification on Swallow Lake Reserve provides a good insight into the full consequences of political favouritism, consequences which are of continuing importance in preventing Indian solidarity in the urban environment. In the

Saskatoon case, Indian migrants from Swallow Lake stem from all the major social groupings on the reserve. The apparently insoluble problems resulting from Indian urbanization cannot be understood unless the political background to family cleavages on the reserve has been spelled out in detail.

## The Swallow Lake Reserve

The Swallow Lake Reserve is located within 150 miles of Saskatoon, and has supplied a large segment of that city's Indian minority. The Reserve itself is large, covering sixty-five square miles, with a population of 840 in 1970. Although the Reserve is not the most advanced in the Province, it is widely recognized as being among the more progressive. Located along the Saskatchewan River, Swallow Lake offers a splendid combination of gentle farmland, rich pasture fields and hunting grounds.

As on most Canadian Indian Reserves, the population is extraordinarily youthful, with almost 60 per cent below the age of 20. The overall income, housing and employment situation is disastrous. Fifty per cent of the employable population had an earned income in 1969 of less than $1,000; another 15 per cent had an earned income in that year of less than $2,000. Figures for Swallow Lake amply support the findings of the *Hawthorn Report* that the vast majority of employable residents are unskilled labourers, farm workers, loggers, and fishermen and domestics. Social assistance encompasses most households on the reserve; it is a safe estimate that welfare payments have far exceeded earnings from gainful employment in the past decade. The bulk of crop and pasture land (27,130 acres) has been leased to neighbouring whites, so that independent Indian farming is practically nonexistent. There is, for example, only one combine on the reserve, and individual Indians own merely 15 old tractors and 20 trucks. Animal stock is limited to 150 beef cattle, 50 horses, and 150 chickens.

An Indian Affairs Branch survey estimated the income from farming (not counting leases) and animal husbandry in 1969 to have been only $17,000 for the entire reserve. There is no mineral resource activity, and no income from a potentially lucrative tourism and recreation industry. The reserve, however, does have a Co-op store, which offers full-time employment to one resident; four school buses are operated by Indians, and four persons are employed by the Band Council.

58

Although the provision of utilities and housing has improved on the reserve, the situation is still far from satisfactory. Ninety-four households out of 135 are supplied with electricity, but there is only one telephone, no sewage disposal system, no indoor plumbing and, surprisingly, no fire protection equipment on the entire reserve. Over half the houses have three rooms or less, and it is estimated that 80 new houses will be required by 1975. Three-quarters of the roads on the reserve are listed as unimproved, the others being gravel; no asphalt roads exist. There are no industrial or maintenance buildings on the reserve, and no medical station. The federal Government has built a six-room school, two barns and three teachers' residences; Indian public buildings are limited to two churches (heavily unused), a community hall, an administration building and a Co-op store.

The Swallow Lake Band has, however, achieved a high level of political and social development, if by that term one refers to the apparent ability of a few families to adapt to the new environment of Indian affairs. The Co-op store itself, one of the few in the Province, is the product of an initiative of the Band Council, which the Indian Affairs Branch was willing to support. Two students from the reserve were enrolled in universities in 1969-70, and two other young people were placed in in-service training in the same year. There is considerable movement between the reserve and urban centres; no fewer than 78 persons received relocation and employment assistance during that fiscal year, and 26 family units live off the reserve. The Band Council has also been active in educational initiatives at the provincial and federal levels: the reserve has its own school committee, and is also represented on provincial school boards and committees. The rewards of all this new activity are confined to a small group that occupies positions of leadership within the reserve. In short, the Swallow Lake Reserve illustrates the dominant feature of reserve life in the Province of Saskatchewan and Canada as a whole: the emergence of a small cadre of leaders in a morass of deprivation and exclusion.

The lines of cleavage on the Swallow Lake Reserve are predictable; they are visible in outline in the earliest stages of reserve history. The study of one large family on the reserve illustrates the factors involved in determining the native power structure.[8]

The Victor Sunderland family migrated to Swallow Lake

from the Winnipeg area, entering the reserve when it was established on January 1, 1879 under the auspices of the Christian Missionary Society. Victor was paid fifty pounds per annum by the Anglican Church as the first teacher. He was also deeply involved with specific Church activity; he was a lay reader for the Church which had a mission nearby, and one of his sons, Robert, took up the leadership after his death.

His descendents point out that the Victor Sunderland family considered itself the most acculturated on the reserve. His choice of marriage partner appears to bear out this conclusion: Mary Douglas, an ambitious Metis girl and a teacher. Agent records of agricultural production during the period show Victor Sunderland to have been the most successful farmer on the reserve. He was also chief headman after Chief White Owl. When Chief White Owl died in 1903, the Agent commented in his report: "Chief White Owl died recently. The leading and most progressive and enterprising members of the band are now Victor Sunderland and his sons, all of whom speak English and aspire to live like white men. . . ."[9]

The Sunderland-Douglas alliance has resulted over the next five generations in a complex kinship system involving the "highest" as well as the "lowest" family groups on the reserve. It encompasses the Nevilles, McKnights and Smiths – with over four hundred members, the largest reserve "family." There are "leading" families among them who have maintained the tradition of Victor Sunderland, but the majority display the conventional symptoms of personal and social disorganization.

The history of the Sunderland family reveals the precariousness of "leading family" status. Far from being a relaxed non-competitive and non-political haven, the reserve has always been a hotbed of politics in which disaster has threatened at every turn. The prize, clearly, was a position of respect and prestige; a mistake meant both impoverishment and permanent exclusion. Family life provided the framework for a Darwinian struggle for survival; "leading family" status could never be taken for granted. Given the facts of political life, very few families could attain this position. Therefore the record of the Sunderland family is dominated by two features: the downward mobility of the vast majority of Victor's descendants, and the success of a few chosen nuclear families.

Four major groupings of families can be distinguished among the lineal descendants of Victor Sunderland and Mary Douglas.

The standard chosen here to differentiate them evaluates family performance according to type and level of dependency on the larger society. The point is not that dependency is "good" or "bad" or that white society is "better," but that dependency is the central fact of life for the Indians, and the principal feature of interchange between the two cultures.

First there are the "leading families" who: 1) farm extensively and raise cattle; 2) have property on the reserve such as large houses and machinery; 3) have earned incomes of over $4,000; and 4) have important positions in reserve government and good contacts with the Indian Affairs Branch. It is interesting that in the late nineteenth century, the IAB used similar criteria to identify specific Indian sub-groupings: neatness; farming; cooperating with "church and state"; family and personal morality; a sense of property.[10] Essentially there are only three nuclear units at the present time in this category: Cynthia Sunderland and Thomas McKnight and their son Robert (and his wife Miriam); Samuel Neville and Lynda McKnight – a daughter of Thomas McKnight and Cynthia Sunderland; and Tom Smith, second-generation descendant of Michael Sunderland, and his wife Jenny Rioux from the Stonewall Reserve, who formed a "leading family" prior to their departure from Swallow Lake Reserve in 1969. It should be emphasized that the Victor Sunderland family is in its sixth generation and stems from a base of 10 children. The casualty rate is obviously rather high.

A second reserve grouping has been labelled "self-supporting." Unlike the "leading" families they (1) do not farm profitably, raise cattle or own modern machinery; nor (2) does their income equal that of the top group. But (3) they do have houses of four rooms or more. Their political connections (4) are not as prestigious. But they do share an essential feature with the "leading" families: they are not wholly supported by welfare. Instead, they derive some earned income from employment on or near the reserve – for example, as Welfare Agents, clerks in the reserve cooperative, and school bus drivers. The limited number of employment possibilities since the establishment of the reserves, and the inherent difficulties in managing viable farming and grazing operations without the wholesale cooperation of the Indian Affairs Branch, have limited the number of Indians who could qualify for this status. At the moment, therefore, there are not even ten households who belong to this sub-grouping.

The third sub-group, the "semi-dependent" includes individuals and families whose welfare dependency, while severe, does alternate with attempts to find work on or off the reserve. They have no household property of value; their income is under $2,000 per annum; they have poor housing and they have little authority on the reserve. Often a family difficulty – illegitimacy, or illness, has been responsible for this low status. It is interesting that "leading" families on the reserve emphasize the messiness of the houses of the "semi-dependent."

The final category, the "confirmed indigent," represent the lowest socio-economic status. At this level there is no desire for gainful employment of any kind, and no aspirations to property ownership. The income level generally remains below $1,000 per family. Some still live in log houses. The IAB is rapidly dismantling them, but the cheap frame houses which replace them are soon wrecks. For the "confirmed indigent," welfare dependency is the norm.

These last two categories, the "indigent" and the "semi-dependent," comprise the majority of the Sunderland clan. The indigent are particularly numerous, accounting for approximately one-half of the total. But the semi-dependent do not conform to the white stereotype of the completely shiftless Indian. They clearly do attempt, from time to time, to achieve economic independence. Given their low reserve status, however, they are relatively unacquainted with the use of money in a competitive society, with handling modern tools and appliances, or with dealing with the outside world. Often shy and retiring, they are particularly ill-equipped to relate effectively to superiors, Indian or white, on or off the reserve.

The different experience of the four groupings on the reserve carries over into the urban environment. There are not merely "Indians" in the Canadian cities, there are various "classes" of Indians, whose life style on the reserve leads to differing expectations and possibilities. The most striking common feature of the "leading" reserve families in the Victor Sunderland line is that they become the *Affluent* Indians in the city. Both on and off the reserve, the members of these families have prospered.

Thus Tom Smith, while on the reserve, was prominent in the reserve government; one of the foremost farmers; and was associated with the development of the reserve cooperative. Upon moving to Saskatoon, he became Educational Director for the Federation of Saskatchewan Indians, and is now involved with the revitalized Friendship Centre in the city. His wife's father is considered to be the best farmer on the Stonewall Reserve. The wife has a university education and was a teacher on the Swallow Lake Reserve for many years. Their children all have high school diplomas and are all living off the reserve.

Thomas McKnight married Victor Sunderland's daughter Cynthia, forming another union between two leading families. Thomas was the son of James McKnight, who fled from Ten Islands Reserve in 1885 because he refused to take part in the North West Rebellion. Along with several other families from Ten Islands such as the Roses, he settled on Swallow Lake Reserve and refused to leave once the smoke had cleared.

Like Victor Sunderland, James McKnight was brought to the attention of the Commissioner of Indian Affairs for his ambition and farming ability. His enterprise was passed on to Thomas and his children. Given the death of Thomas McKnight and the departure of Tom Smith, Robert and Lynda became the nucleus of the two "leading families" in the extended family system.

Robert married an ambitious Metis by the name of Miriam Maheux. Lynda McKnight, Thomas' daughter, married his hired man, James Neville. In Robert's family, Bruce, Edgar, Rosemarie and Barbara have left the reserve and are doing very well indeed in various urban centres. Bruce is the Communications Consultant for the Federation of Saskatchewan Indians (FSI), and was a constable in the Prince Albert Police Force – one of the young Indians in the province who has already made a name for himself in Indian Affairs. His brother Ken has taken over his parents' farm on the reserve. Mildred and Florence, two daughters, are on the reserve with large families; although they have not equalled the reputation of their brothers and sisters, they are ensuring an advanced education for their children. Harold, on the other hand, is reported to have married a "bad woman" and has fallen by the wayside.

In every "leading family" in the Victor Sunderland kinship system, there have been strong women – either Metis or from other "leading families" on or off the reserve. Men without determined wives have invariably fallen by the wayside. Ideally in a leading family, a strong woman is matched with a farmer who similarly values saving and production and enjoys the full support of the IAB. The evidence from the Swallow Lake Reserve would seem to support the conclusion of students of acculturation, who are impressed with the resilience of Indian women in culture change situations.[11]

The role of women in variations of family patterns on the reserve is striking at all levels. Among the well-off Indians, Cynthia Sunderland, Jenny Rioux, Miriam Maheux and Lynda McKnight have been decisive in assisting their husbands in maintaining habits of saving and transmitting them to their children. Thus Miriam McKnight, Robert's wife, is able to check the devastation of indigent relatives, both Metis and Indian, by keeping a close eye on grocery expenditures. At a certain point, no more food is made available and the relatives must either leave or find another, more pliant family for their meals. Reserve relatives in the McKnight extended family now stay for only one meal, and then go away. Similarly, the Bruce McKnight and Tom Smith families are not overwhelmed by distant relatives, because a different socialization experience has created distinct expectations from these families.[12]

## The "Leading Families" in the City

The strategy of assimilation pursued by Indian Affairs on the reserves failed. To be sure, some Indians were enfranchised, choosing the white world and sometimes surviving in it – often becoming the most vociferous critics of Indian culture and tradition. Evidence from selected reserves suggests that the high point of this movement ended around the time of the First World War.

But the numbers remained insignificant. Essentially, the success of the policy depended on a rate of enfranchisement which exceeded the population growth. Disease and poverty reduced the population in the decades after Treaty, and it seemed for a while that the IAB had a fighting chance. But after 1945 the population growth got completely out of hand. The "leading families" could no longer fulfill their colonial role on the reserves.

But the IAB had been succesful in creating a leadership cadre of "leading families" on many reserves. These families had long been acquainted with one another; there had been many intermarriages among them from one reserve to the next. When the individual biographies of the *Affluent* Indians in Saskatoon are studied, it becomes clear that they had interacted long before they moved to the city. For generations, the "leading families" had worked with the Government as brokers in the field of Indian Affairs; in so doing they associated with their peers from other reserves. It was inevitable that members of the "leading families" would be drawn to the city. First the formal governmental agencies at federal and provincial levels were being "Indianized" and were desperately short of qualified personnel. Since these offices were located mainly in the cities, the obvious result was migration from the reserves.

Indeed the migration patterns to Saskatoon from individual reserves can be explained to a large extent by the movement of the "leading families." Thus when David Ahenakew, presently Chief of the Federation of Saskatchewan Indians became a Placement officer with the Indian-Metis Branch in 1967, the example of his successful experience persuaded many other families and individuals from his reserve to try their luck in Saskatoon as well.

Second, the revival of Indian consciousness in Canada carried with it a demand for native organizations to represent the interests of that Indian-Metis constituency. The "leading families" assumed the mantle of leadership as a matter of course. Some of the (numerous) native bodies such as the Federation of Saskatchewan Indians have become extremely large, with a Central Staff, regional offices, and teams of field workers for the 67 bands in the Province. Since the organizations operate out of the larger urban Centres, most of the full-time employees bring their families with them from the reserve. In both cases, demands for Indian personnel coincided with material and ideological incentives to draw the reserve elite into relocation programs.

Once in the city, the leading families coalesce into the hard social formation of the *Affluent*. Under the pressure of the urban environment, they develop something different from their reserve "leading family" status. On the Swallow Lake Reserve, the residence pattern does not show a rigid residential separation between this group and other families, or the total absence of interaction between the "leading families" and the poorer people. In Saskatoon, on the other hand, residential separation is obvious. Given the various arteries into the IAB and IMB offices it is not necessary to see much of the West Side.

In Saskatoon, the *Affluent* have no meaningful contact with the rank and file Indians and Metis. There is a great deal of interaction over the counters of the Indian Affairs Branch, the Indian-Metis Branch, and the Department of Welfare, where considerable numbers of the *Affluent* are employed, but it is restricted to this bleak bureaucratic ritual. Extra-bureaucratic association with native people other than the *Affluent* living in the city is rare. They know few poor Indians in the city other than those who came from their reserve, and they do not associate even with these. Attendance at formal gatherings and meetings reveals even less association between the *Affluent* and the other Indian groupings in town. The latter are never present. Even more important, the *Affluent* have as little concrete information about the actual living conditions of the poor Indians in the city as their white counterparts in the bureaucracies. The *Affluent* are the "leaders" in the city; their interests are highly selective and drive deeper the wedge separating them from their native brothers.

## Conclusion

The reserve experience was highly fragmenting, encouraging the growth of an identifiable clientele group. With the revival of Indian consciousness in the 1960s, this group became the spokesman for the Indian people. In so doing, these individuals and families have taken influential positions in agencies and organizations purporting to advance the cause of the native people as a whole. But in the cities they have little contact with other Indians and Metis; a great gap separates the *Affluent* from the rank and file. It is not inappropriate to speak of an "Indian bourgeoisie."

---

[1] "Acculturation" refers to those changes set in motion by the coming together of societies with different cultural traditions. The definition rejects a popular usage equating "acculturation" with "assimilation." There is, needless to say, an enormous literature on ethnicity in North American cities.

[2] Much more detailed studies would be necessary to show that the extended family relations of the *Affluent* Indians and Metis form a more important part of their lives than similar patterns among other ethnic groups in Saskatoon – e.g. the Ukrainians. The decisive characteristic, however, is the stability of the immediate nuclear group and the ease with which this group incorporates the demands of kinship.

[3] Jane Richardson Hanks and Lucien M. Hanks, *Tribe Under Trust*. Toronto, University of Toronto Press, 1950, pp. 45-46. Note also Canadian *Sessional Papers* (House of Commons) 1900, p. 153.

[4] See Michael Harrington, *The Other America*, New York, Macmillan, 1962.

[5] *Hawthorn Report*, Vol. 1, p. 116.

[6] See *Indian-Eskimo Association of Canada Bulletin*, Vol. 8, No. 4, October, 1967, p. 4.

[7] *Hawthorn Report*, Vol. 1, p. 129.

[8] The names of the reserve and band members have been altered.

[9] "Victor Sunderland No. 2 and his son Edward had four acres of oats, five of wheat and two of barley; good crops and ready for cutting; garden was in better condition than I ever found it, also the house, and the place around was cleaned up, a great improvement on what it used to be. I complimented him on the change, and expressed the hope that he would continue to keep it in such good order; that, being a headman, he should be an example for the others. Sunderland has one or two boys at Emmanuel College, Prince Albert."Canada, *Sessional Papers* (House of Commons), *Agent Reports*, 1897, p. 249.

[10] Canada, *Sessional Papers* (House of Commons), 1897, p. 198. Also Hanks and Hanks, *op. cit.*, pp. 155-159.

[11] Hanks and Hanks, *op. cit.*; William Caudill, "Psychological Characteristics of Acculturated Wisconsin Ojibwa Children," *American Anthropologist*, Vol. 50, 1949, pp. 409-427; Harry Alkin, "The Northern Arapaho of Wyoming," in Ralph Linton, ed., *Acculturation in Seven American Indian Tribes*, New York, Peter Smith, 1940; Natalie F. Joffee, "The Fox of Iowa," in Linton, Cf. Louise and George Spindler, "Male and Female Adaptations in Culture Change," *American Anthropologist*, Vol. 60, 1950, p. 217:
> Menomini males appear to be more anxious and less controlled than do the women. And the women are psychologically more conservative. This suggests that for some reason the disruptions created in rapid culture change hit the men more directly, leaving the women less changed and anxious.

[12] It appears that education has not been a decisive variable in assisting the leading families in the Victor Sunderland clan. Victor Sunderland and Mary Douglas were both teachers and were concerned to send their children to school. But Thomas McKnight is well known to have had a miserable time of it in school; he never did learn English and an interpreter was necessary when he spoke with outsiders or the Indian Agent. The same is true with his son Robert and his wife Miriam. Robert has perhaps a Grade II education and can scarcely read or write; Miriam has no education whatsoever. Although they emphasized the value of education to their children, the latter have had a great deal of difficulty in obtaining a Grade XII education. In Saskatchewan this is not generally considered to be a notable achievement. Tom Smith was also able to obtain only a Grade II education, but his ability to farm does not seem to have been impaired. On the other hand, the Roses, a classic dependent family on the reserve, are noted for ease of learning coupled with absence of motivation.

# 3
## The Logic of Skid Row

The *Welfare* Indians and Metis form the largest and fastest growing native grouping in the city. The term does not necessarily mean that *Welfare* Indians are permanently on the receiving end of official provincial welfare services. Only at certain times might they qualify for this assistance; many never will. Rather, the *Welfare* segment of the native population in Saskatoon is defined by its basic opposition to the urban value system as a whole, particularly its emphasis on "middle class" thrift. Living on skid row, the *Welfare* Indians are permanently alienated. Part-time jobs may supplement income from welfare, voluntary programs for the urban indigent, theft and begging. But the rejection of industrial life is total; *Welfare* Indians are defined by this decision, as well as by the extreme dependence and peripheral status that it implies. The *Welfare* Indians and Metis are best differentiated from the *Affluent* by considering the same variables used when describing the latter.

### 1. Jobs
The *Welfare* category by definition does not have stable employment. However, unless single men are completely unemployable, they have considerable difficulty in obtaining assistance from the Department of Welfare, and therefore are likely to drop by the Indian Affairs Branch or the provincial Indian-Metis Branch to see about job openings. Accepting a job ensures assistance for at least two weeks, and very likely for a full month, from the IAB. The possibility of unemployment insurance serves as an incentive to keep a job for a while.[1] If they have no friends to stay with, they can stay at the Salvation Army for three days, using up meal tickets or eating at the Friendship Inn two blocks away, in

the hope that something – a good friend for example – will turn up in that period. The job turnover of this group is extraordinarily high: many leave after a week; some quit after three days. A follow-up study of thirty individuals produced an average job tenure of three weeks. *These represent the aristocracy of the Welfare class.*[2]

Unmarried mothers with children stand a far better chance with the Department of Welfare. Indeed, welfare rates appear to favour having two or more illegitimate children. Of 104 native families who obtained counselling and welfare assistance from the Salvation Army Family Services Office, 50 per cent were unmarried mothers and 31 of the latter had three or more children; only eight had one child. Salvation Army assistance of this kind is in excess of provincial Welfare (whose files are closed), but the Army's files list the value of welfare cheques received by its clientele. More children mean more money. Although another child adds to household expenses it is more than possible that the mother "gains" by the margin.[3]

The job market for native girls with a low educational level is extraordinarily bleak. In the years 1967-1969, of 215 women who applied at the Indian Affairs Branch for jobs, 124 were placed as domestics and 48 as waitresses, often in the seediest establishments on the West Side. Not surprisingly, many women appear not to have considered the possibility of employment, given the certainty of low earnings on the one hand, and the necessity of finding a baby-sitter on the other. Typical of this sample is a girl who came to Saskatoon to live with her sister some years ago with one illegitimate child, and rapidly expanded her family to a total of five. Two children were given away, but she was still left with an allowance of $178 per month from the Department of Welfare. She could not hope to clear that sum from "gainful employment." Of the sample, well over 50 per cent took no interest in jobs – either permanent or short term.[4]

## 2. Housing – the "Hidden" Poor

Most Indians and Metis of this stratum are seen in a rather small and circumscribed part of the city known to the local inhabitants as the West Side. It extends along 20th Street from Avenue E uptown to 2nd Avenue, but also includes the adjacent streets. Railway yards used to lie in the area between 1st Avenue and Idylwyld Avenue a critical sociological division. The former area was the respectable business district of Saskatoon; the latter

69

encompassed the city's Bowery. The removal of the yards has had two important consequences: first, the liberated area has been transformed into one of the most modern shopping centres in North America, so that the centre of gravity of the business establishment has shifted to the West, threatening to reform 20th Street. Second, while sin thus far still survives on 20th Street, drinking and gaming have gained a toehold around 1st and 2nd Avenues.

All along this area lie the bars, cafes and poolrooms that the solid citizens of Saskatoon associate with the less desirable: the Barry and the Albany, the Saskatoon and the Queens, etc. The Salvation Army Hostel and adjacent Thrift Store, located a block away from the Barry Hotel and the China Lamp Café, cast their long shadows across 20th Street and confirm the judgment of the Betters. It is worth pointing out that the *Affluent* Indians share the general view that the area is teeming with sin and corruption, and that the Indians and Metis involved have succumbed to liquor and other conventional forms of vice.

One might have expected a great many Indians to live in the area, which contains large numbers of housing units, many of which are substandard. The best-informed social workers and program administrators had predicted that a house-to-house survey would turn up native people by the hundreds. It is worth recalling the old adage that people never are where you think they are. A survey report which was written in August of 1969 merits quoting in detail since it conveys some of the flavour of the hard-core West Side:

> The area covered today consisted in the 100, 200 and 300 blocks on 20th Street, both sides, and Avenues B and C between 19th and 20th Streets. Other areas considered covered were those in the first three blocks on 19th Street, which appeared to be only vacant lots and business establishments with no living quarters at the rear.
>
> Perhaps the most startling fact apparent was the total lack of animosity directed towards Indian people in general (with the exception of several disgruntled store owners with whom Indians had outstanding accounts). The fact that there were actually very few Indians residing in this specific area (above and behind business establishments) likely accounts for this. White proprietors seemed to accept as a matter of course that many Indians hung out in this area but when questioned

about the areas in which the Indians lived, whites were non-committal and vague. I suspect that the business people simply assume that Indians crawl out of the woodwork when the sun goes down.

Empty second stories of buildings are not uncommon. The projected redevelopment of this area of town following the building of the Mid-Town Plaza has created this to some extent; owners assume that their buildings will have to go in the near future and aren't bothering to maintain living quarters. On 20th specifically, apartments rented out were inhabited by numerous families of Chinese, Greeks and white trash, the latter category outnumbering all other residents by far. On 20th, I found only one rather loose family unit (two ladies reeking of easy virtue, two children and one man) and an Indian woman married to a white apartment caretaker.

The apartment blocks of B and C (300 block south), which we expected to be rampant with Indians, were curiously quiet and pleasant. With the exception of a fine old couple and a relative who lived with them (and the possibility of two or three single men), the tenants of these apartments were primarily white male pensioners. Houses in this area were owned or rented by Chinese families.

Although hostility towards Indians appeared subdued, there was, at least implicitly, a move to keep Indian tenants out of this area – landlords preferred pensioners, foreigners and a rather low white element. Proprietors, generally landlords, seemed to feel that as long as the Indians bought in their stores they were all right – and a large percentage of trade in this area does come from Indians. But they don't by and large live there – 12 to 15 is the maximum number located at this point.

An interesting, although possibly irrelevant footnote here is the fact that, according to the proprietor of the Barry Hotel, the Indian prostitutes have moved out and been replaced by white girls. They've all gone somewhere, but where?[5]

Eventually the Indian minority was found, more than 300 households strong, residing in the poorest dwellings but not at the moment in any one concentration. Thus the pattern so far is based on the slum dwelling rather than the firmly-established racial slum. There are, however, unmistakable and disturbing trends evident in the latter direction.

Until 1969, when a general economic slow-down set in in the province of Saskatchewan, the city of Saskatoon had enjoyed a half-decade of unparalleled prosperity and economic activity. The value of real estate doubled during the period, and produced a constant flux on the market, before which the Indian minority was completely helpless. The removal of CNR rail lines and offices from the heart of the city threw open a rich area for development. Similarly, the announcement by Gulf Oil that it was closing the refinery on the West Side may have been disturbing to the employees, but it had the same effect of liberating a formerly untouchable area for home construction. Even in anticipation, Weldon Street, adjacent to the refinery, which for years had languished in shacks embedded in an unbearable stench, underwent a transformation. The number of outhouses fell by 50 per cent within a year. New houses appeared. But ominously, rents rose to put pressure on the pockets of the hard-core poor. Two years ago, it was one "Indian Street."

Essentially, the Indian *lumpenproletariat* has been too miserable to be able to develop a solid slum. Indian and Metis families simply pick up the worst and cheapest dwelling that the European immigrant families leave behind when they move to the suburbs. There is a tendency for other Indian families to join it in neighbouring shacks if they also should come free. The characteristic feature of bad housing on the West Side is a series of shacks in a row on a street, but usually not far from better homes with lawns and gardens. During the years of the boom, the value of the land under the shacks skyrocketed, and many were bought up, torn down, and replaced by duplexes. Where this happened, the Indians had to move out. The outer perimeter of the West Side, in particular, has shown many examples of this housing situation in the past few years.

However, the general economic slow-down in the province and the tailing off in the construction industry may drastically change the real estate market. The trend in the past year has been a drift of the native population toward areas that could easily become hard-core racial slums. Thus, for example, the cheap apartments above stores on 2nd Avenue will not revive in value as the business area shifts farther east toward the Mid-Town Plaza. Already, businessmen who cannot move their store locations are concerned by the decline on 2nd Avenue. Similarly, the movement beyond 33rd Street on 1st and 2nd Avenue is ominous, for the largest collection of war-time shacks exists in this area. Saskatchewan Avenue, although mercifully short, is already hard-core slum district, characteristically well-hidden from the public eye. There are also areas on the West Side which are showing signs of extreme decay and which will not be much affected by the shift in the business centre. Thus the Avenue L and M districts below 33rd Street (and again immediately about 22nd Street), as well as the region south of 20th (Avenues G and H) could succumb to a worse condition than that existing today. The bulk of the native poor already live around these areas; the drift is toward them. No clearer indication could be found than the shift of the prostitution centres toward these same districts. The proprietor of the Barry Hotel was not quite correct; there is still one establishment specializing in Indian women in his neighbourhood. But only one. The others have gone to new homes with the *Welfare* Indians.

## 3. *Family Life*

If the most striking characteristic of the *Affluent* Indian and Metis families was the primacy of the nuclear family and the supporting role of extended family relationships, the complete breakdown of family life is apparent among the *Welfare* Indians and Metis.

The "indigent" on the reserve included some families who had chosen not to accept a competitive life-style. Although desperately poor, they retained a strong sense of dignity and family solidarity, and placed great stress on affection and child-centredness both in the immediate nuclear family and in the extended family. This variety of family cannot leave the protection of the reserve, and it does not feed the ranks of the urban *Welfare* Indians. The latter derive from "indigents" whose family life has disintegrated on the reserve, and who have been socialized to take for granted a large number of immediate relationships considered deviant both by other Indians and by the larger society.

It is inappropriate to linger with prurient interest on the details of illegitimacy or prostitution and the like, when these have been explored in many previous studies.[6] It is a safe estimate that family life in the group leaves something to be desired, and case studies easily confirm this generalization. Large numbers of transient relatives and friends roam about at the expense of stability and discipline of any kind whatsoever. In one case, all five illegitimate children of a woman were from different fathers, and three were almost certainly conceived in front of the eyes of the small children. It is not that the extended family concept is preferred to the nuclear family. Neither social formation serves any function other than immediate gratification at this level of disintegration; in fact, neither truly exists. Uninhibited passion and unrestrained violence have destroyed any semblance of family solidarity.[7]

## 4. Personal Disintegration

Although the evidence for the breakdown of family life in the city is very good, generalizations concerning personal disintegration among the urban native *Welfare* grouping are far more hazardous. Relatively careful studies of specific reserves have been carried out both in Canada and in the United States on this subject.[8] The specific impact of city life, however, has yet to be measured. Interviews and case studies do not provide a sufficient basis for conclusions about relative percentages. Indian Affairs Branch officials estimate the unemployment rate to be above 60 per cent for native people in the city. About 50 per cent of the Salvation Army clientele is native, and the use of this institution is widely associated in the *white community* as a sign of breakdown. Alcoholism is obviously a problem; indeed the Indians of Saskatoon were partially responsible for a piece of legal reform: the number actually desiring confinement for a month became so great that drunkenness had to be eliminated as a criminal offence.

Exact statistics on legal offences committed by native people in Saskatoon could not be assembled. Criminal records are closed, and without a careful study of individual cases, it would be impossible to disentangle ignorance of the law and discrimination from actual criminal intent resulting in arrest and convictions. The overall direction of the evidence is clear enough. It is possible to conclude that a very high level of personal disorganization exists according to the standards generally employed, but it cannot be demonstrated that it is higher in the city than on the reserves, or vice versa.

## 5. Identity in the City

According to white standards, the *Welfare* Indians and Metis are objectively oppressed. No survey is required to know that the dwellings are substandard. The dismal exteriors of slum apartments and shacks do not hide fresh, comfortable interiors. Welfare assistance in Saskatoon is not lavish. Many of the welfare

74

payments are so low that it must be extremely difficult for women and their children to manage. For three children, the rate rarely rises above $200, and in some cases is considerably below that figure. In one instance, an unmarried mother with five children had a monthly allowance of $170. At this level of income, it is possible to eke out only a bare level of subsistence.[9]

Observers of Indian slums have invariably been led to stress the irreversibility and destructive effect of poverty on the individual character of the native people. They implicitly emphasize the need for better guidance and control, presumably to bring the standard of living closer to that of the middle class. There is a great danger in this point of view, which so clearly reflects an ideological preference. An opposing evaluation, which characterizes the urban Indian and the Metis *Welfare* grouping as evil, mean, violent, brutish and criminal, reflects the interests of a specific political group. Skid row has its own structure and rationale, and offers rewards which should not be underestimated or casually dismissed as false consciousness.

On the fringes of skid row there are indeed many individual native males, in particular, who appear isolated and lonesome, sitting out the night on the steps of the Salvation Army Hostel or on a stool of the China Lamp Café. But among the hard-core *Welfare* Indians and Metis, alongside family violence, illegitimacy and the rest, there is a vibrant social life centring around the "Indian Houses" that serve as informal clearinghouses for the group. Although poor, these small establishments are well known as entertainment centres among the native people. One house on the West Side remains a haven for Indians from a Northern Agency – an all-Indian place to drink and party. Indeed, when the neighbouring houses were abandoned, it became for a while a major social centre. During the time when the first Friendship Centre in Saskatoon was failing for lack of Indian clientele, an hour's notice could draw fifty to a hundred Indians into a tiny three-room shack for an all-night bash. Similarly, certain hotels – the Baldwin, the Queens, the Barry – are very popular prenocturnal bars. There is, in short, a great deal of social interaction and community spirit among the *Welfare* native people.

Case studies of individuals reinforce the conclusion that alienation is not a major problem in this grouping. The life-style may be distasteful in the view of the white middle class or the *Affluent* Indians. The human cost for children is very high, judging from the school reports of the children of the more active members of this group. The girl with five illegitimate children is scarcely lost in a sea of loneliness and despair. She eagerly awaits the evening, when she disappears from her base-ment suite, nonchalantly assuming that the people upstairs will look after her children. There is no absence of white trash to buy drinks; indeed, the youngest child is every ounce the off-spring of this low-white class: mean-looking and coarse-featured.

The researcher would be hard put to substantiate a claim that the city slum is objectively more dislocating for indigent Indians or Metis than are the reserves. Born and brought up on welfare, indigent Indians and Metis are hardly demoralized by continued reliance on it in the city. Provided that assistance from the Department of Social Welfare can be obtained, the balance of advantages in very many cases would appear to lie in the urban environment.

The reserve is clearly a less demanding enclave, where there is far less trouble with social workers, police, and outraged landlords; but it is also a far less interesting location. The night life of Saskatoon may not match that of New York or London; but when measured against the standards of Kinistino, Indian Head or Moose Jaw, the titillations are nothing short of spectac-ular.

### Pan-Indianism on Skid Row

As with the *Affluent*, a Pan-Indianism emerges at the lowest social level in the Indian community to bolster a sense of identi-ty. The all-night parties of the *Welfare* Indians rarely include a white man. However, association with poor whites goes on infor-mally in bars until closing time, and sexual play is very common with the rather more dilapidated Indian women. Indeed, at this level, Indians and non-Indians share a common life-style.[10]

Some observers have made much of the interaction that goes on between whites and Indians at the skid row level. Neither group is concerned about financial solvency; their common socio-economic status willy-nilly induces collaboration in survival on skid row. The white "disreputable poor" is as marginal as the Indian. Patterns of dependence are mutual.[11]

At the same time, there is ambivalence and tension between the two groups. Whites on skid row are, at least, verbally as racist as the white middle class. Indians are inferior, lazy, untrust-worthy drunks.

We find in the attitude of the skid row white, therefore, three principal ingredients: first, the Indian is regarded as a bum; second, he is regarded as unreliable; third, he is regarded as unduly violent. But we also find that in practice the whites do many 'jobs' with Indians: whites have Indian girl-friends, with whom they cooperate for the purposes of hustling and petty theft; much drinking is done by whites and Indians jointly. It is evident that there is considerable divergence between protestation and practice.[12]

It seems fair to say that the possibility of relatively easy association with whites constitutes an important attraction of skid row for migrant Indians. But relationships among Indians remain the most important factor of community life for the skid row native.

Despite the constant movement, a definable *Welfare* grouping is solidifying in the city. The evidence suggests that the hard-core of the larger *Welfare* community is made up of the unmarried women and their children who have certain access to steady welfare assistance, and who are in a position to live with men on a common-law basis. Together with a growing number of unstable Indian and Metis family units that have migrated to and taken up what appears to be permanent residence in Saskatoon, this group has a vested interest in living in the city.

As more and more Indians and Metis discover the city, increasing numbers tend to stay there for longer intervals, gradually becoming part of the *Welfare* community. The availability of accommodation at the Salvation Army or with friends, along with the welfare services provided by the various agencies and the free food dispensed by the Friendship Inn, provide a cushion for the unplanned growth of the *Welfare* grouping. As the number of resident native people increases, there are greater possibilities for finding accommodation for at least short periods of time, and for finding food to supplement that offered by the voluntary programs. Essentially the slum conditions of the reserve are extended into the city and given a pan-Indian setting.

### Internal Exiles: The Welfare on the Reserve

As with the *Affluent*, the *Welfare* families and individuals are identifiable on the reserve. On the Swallow Lake Reserve we have noted that roughly half of the descendents of Victor Sunderland are "confirmed indigents," who have never tried to improve their standard of living. At this level on the reserve, and

77

in sharp contrast to the "leading families," there is no desire for gainful employment of any kind, and no aspirations to property ownership. Entire family sub-groupings subsist entirely on welfare, as the previous generations subsisted on rations.

The "confirmed indigent," therefore, represent the antithesis of the "leading families" on the Swallow Lake Reserve. They have accepted welfare dependence and all that goes with it: family breakdown, unsanitary living conditions, bad housing, and the happy-go-lucky life in general. They have accepted failure as defined by the larger society, and move logically to skid row from the reserve. Indeed, migrants of this class from the Swallow Lake Reserve have adapted easily to welfare dependency in Saskatoon. Apart from trouble with landlords and welfare workers, they appear to be quite content in the urban environment: they participate in the social events of the *Welfare* grouping, remain in Saskatoon as long as the balance of advantages favours them, and then return to the reserve.

Individual case-studies of migrant *Welfare* Indians quickly become repetitive, monotonously underscoring the fact that life in the city is identical with that on the reserve. Whether Bruce Neville leans against a tree on the Swallow Lake Reserve or a lamp-post in Saskatoon, the motivation and consequences are unlikely to be different. Whether he drinks with friends on the reserve or friends in the city, the rationale and results are identical. They are even likely to be the same friends.

On the Swallow Lake Reserve the chief behaviour patterns associated with skid row are apparent. This is particularly the case with the use of alcohol. Just as it is impossible to imagine the *Welfare* without reference to drinking, so also does much of the life of the "confirmed indigents" centre around liquor. The very similarity of alcoholism on the reserve and the city demands that the personal disorganization and deviance among the *Welfare* and "confirmed indigent" be analyzed with some care. Among the *Welfare* it is simply absurd to argue that drinking is a reaction to the crisis of adjustment to the urban environment. Among the "confirmed indigent" on the Swallow Lake Reserve, alcoholism is not a product of the strains of competition within the community. In both cases, for the *Welfare* and the "confirmed indigent," deviance performs a function. A behaviour pattern such as drinking cannot be isolated from this context. We have already noted this function on skid row in Saskatoon.

The chief compensation of skid row for Indians is that it

permits community life *outside the norms of the larger society*. Thus several authors have been surprised that the solitary Indian drunk is an exception, and that drinking among Indians is intensely social.[13] But it is not at all surprising, if the basic hostility between the *Welfare* sub-culture and the institutions of city life are kept in mind. For only on skid row can Indians unite with each other, and to a certain extent, with the white poor, in protest against a society which has emasculated them. Respectable whites may loath skid row and public drunkenness – so much the better. "Indians have perfectly logical and understandable reasons to drink."[14]

The "confirmed indigent" on the reserve move to the urban skid row if and when it offers more community advantages than life on the isolated reserve. But their style of life does not change. In either case, however, they are deviants in terms of the larger society; in either case they suffer extreme deprivation. But before taking away the bottle, it is necessary to be clear about the reasons why the "confirmed indigent" make up a majority of the reserve Indians. They are failures by their own admission. And slum existence is miserable, especially in the Canadian winter. There is no need to be prosaic about a community of extreme poverty. Whatever excitement there may be is purchased at a high price.

## The Philosophy of Reserve Welfare

Essentially, any satisfactory analysis of the "confirmed indigents" on the reserve must extend beyond biographical detail to an examination of the administration of Indian Affairs in Canada. The prevailing explanation of poverty in this group, which views it in terms of the personal inadequacy, wickedness or inferiority, fails to satisfy the most elementary curiosity about this lamentable situation.

The brute facts are overwhelming: many entire reserves even worse off than Swallow Lake, with practically every household on welfare; functional illiteracy throughout the reserves of the North; tuberculosis flourishing; malnutrition and near starvation in the destitute Indian and Metis communitites. The Indian population is almost certainly worse off today, in real terms, than it was two hundred years ago. The "leading families" on the reserves may have benefited, relatively speaking, from their link with the Indian Affairs Branch; the others, particularly the least powerful, were trapped early in the game, and were broken.

79

Given the control of the Indian administration over the lives of the Indian population, relief and welfare policy offer a vivid example of the inadequacies of government negligence in this area. Following the original establishment of the reserves, the economic situation of most Indian bands was desperate and relief and rations were distributed. But this was not seen as a desirable or permanent arrangement. Rather, "self-support" was emphasized. Agent *Reports* continually repeated the elusive goal. For example in 1881:

> I do not wish to be too sanguine, but if progression goes on next year at the same rate as it has since last spring, I have every confidence that the Indians who settle on reserves in this district will be self-supporting.[15]

To no avail. The native population could not be fed and clothed on the income derived from traditional occupations such as hunting and fishing, supplemented by farming and animal husbandry. Relief, therefore became a permanent feature of Indian Affairs policy, extended more or less stringently as the day-to-day budgetary needs of the federal Government dictated.

The Great Depression was a landmark in the development of a coherent welfare system out of the primitive welfare systems of the early part of the century (even though the Indians remained under a different system). The magnitude of the industrial failure revealed that poverty *within the entire economy* was simply part of the system.[16]

Since the Depression one point in particular about poverty in Canada has become increasingly clear, and links Indian poverty with the overall welfare problem. *Economic growth does not reduce poverty among internal exiles such as the Indians.* The "confirmed indigent" have demonstrated the "new" poverty for a full century. Not just Indians who are aged or disabled, but Indians as a group have been raised in a technologically backward world, and have grown progressively poorer in relation to the settler society around them. Rapid economic development, in short, has worked against the Indians living on or off the reserves.

The gap is now so great and growing so rapidly that Indians as a whole will not "catch up," through the "normal" channels of work and education. More educated Indians, in short, will face skill demands in the economy far beyond the high school level – now considered an unusual achievement for an Indian. In the field of education the gap is growing rapidly: poverty among Indians is unusually hardy, structurally embedded in our society.

Yet official Government programs still aim at the self-support philosophy.

> The insistence by the Branch that the Indian must make some contribution towards his new home (on the reserve) falls into line naturally with the overall policy of developing leadership and responsibility among the Indian people.[17]

Moreover, there is general concern in the larger society that the provision of increased welfare benefits has corrupted the Indians and Metis and undermined their motivation to work for a living. In fact the charge is indicative of a public mood which refuses to recognize the hopelessness of poverty among native people. The provision of relief does not appear to affect employment *where there is work*. Only where the alternative to subsistence relief was subsistence and exhausting work such as trapping, did the extension of relief change work habits, and even then the evidence is mixed.[18]

The Indians and Metis, internal exiles, have faced an almost unbearable future for a hundred years. The effects have been devastating. The "confirmed indigent" are a measure of that tragedy.

### Conclusion: A Native Culture of Poverty?

The term "culture of poverty" has crept into the discussion. I am not happy with it: to Conservatives it serves as an argument to defend inaction. Cultures or "cultural values" must be seen, not as THINGS or real objects that take root and grow; but as convenient abstractions that help describe the way people live under different situations. A "culture of poverty" does not exist as a separate entity. It may help to show why certain groups of people choose a certain way of living *because there is no alternative*. Indians on skid row do not have a genetic composition low on "aspiration," nor is there some Indian "cultural" value of sloth. Skid row is what it is because the larger society must have a place for cast-offs.

According to Michael Harrington, writing about poverty in the United States:

... the most important point is that poverty in America forms a culture, a way of life and feeling, that it makes a whole. It is crucial to generalize this idea, for it profoundly affects how one moves to destroy poverty.[19]

In the Indian case it is particularly important for the white layman to understand poverty as a way of life. The pressures that maintain this situation are unique: the organization of the reserves, the availability of slum life on the reserve as well as the city; the reinforcing character of welfare dependency on the reserve and in the city; and the fundamental conflict between Indians and the larger society. The free-enterprise society in which we live, and the welfare system which reinforces liberal values, are simply not capable of dealing with Indians and skid row, just as they have failed in their policies on the reserves. Unless the drive for money, power and prestige as the predominant mode of competitive behaviour is challenged, the logic of the system will structure the urban native community around skid row. That is precisely what is happening today.

The Welfare Officers and Indian Affairs Officials see what is going on, but cannot arrest the decline. They wish they could speak to a different population at a different time when the ethnic groups could make their way up by saving and hard work. They still invoke the ritual and cite examples. But times and faces have changed.

---

[1] In Saskatchewan, insurance benefits are paid out if the applicant has worked thirty weeks within the last two years and eight weeks within the last twelve months, at jobs where stamps have been sent in regularly. The amount of benefit is calculated on the average of the last thirty contributions. The maximum amount for a married man with children is $53.00 per week. The length of the period of insurance benefits is calculated at a rate of one week for every two weeks in which stamps were paid. (Unemployment Insurance Commission, *Interview*, April 16, 1970.)

[2] Saskatchewan, Department of Indian-Metis Affairs, *IMB Placement Files*.

[3] *Salvation Army Welfare Files*, Saskatoon, Saskatchewan, 1969.

[4] *Salvation Army Welfare Files*, cross-checked with *IAB Placement Officer Reports*.

[5] *Housing Survey Report*, West Side Area File, August, 1969. Personal survey done by C. Klein.

[6] For example, Dunning, "Some Problems of Reserve Indian Communities," *op. cit.*, pp. 24-28; and Davis, *op. cit.*, p. 103.

[7] This does not mean to imply that the breakdown of Indian and Metis families is any worse or more violent than that of other ethnic groups in similar socio-economic circumstances. It merely implies that at that level discipline in the smallest social unit, the family, is practically nil.

[8] See for example L. H. Dizmang, "Suicide Among the Cheyenne Indians," *Bulletin of Suicidology*, Vol. 8, No. 11, July, 1967; M. L. Sievers, "Cigarette and Alcohol Usage Among Southwestern Indians," *American Journal of Public Health*, Vol. 58, No. 71, January, 1968; R. Kuttner, H. Lormez, "Alcohol and Addiction," *Mental Hygiene*, Vol. 51, October, 1967; Daniel Beveridge, *The Socio-Economical Correlates of Economic Dependence in Four Dakota (Sioux) Communities in Saskatchewan*, unpublished Master's Thesis, University of Saskatchewan, April, 1964; *Hawthorn Report*, Vol. 1, pp. 101-145.

[9] *Salvation Army Welfare Files*. As indicated above, however, the allowances may permit a higher income than on the reserve.

[10] See Hugh Brody, *Indians in Skid Row*, N.S.R.E. Department of Indian Affairs and Northern Development, Ottawa, February, 1971, whose conclusions closely parallel mine.

[11] Brody, *op. cit.*, pp. 46-48.

[12] *Ibid.*, p. 48.

[13] Brody, *op. cit.*, p. 13.

[14] Heather Robertson, *Reservations Are For Indians*, Toronto, James Lewis and Samuel, 1970, p. 275.

[15] Quoted in Harper, "Canada's Indian Administration: Basic Concepts and Objectives," p. 121.

[16] T. Lowi, *The End of Liberalism*, New York, W. W. Norton, 1969, p. 216.

[17] E. Fairclough, "Indian Affairs in 1960," *Monetary Times Annual*, (1960), p. 40.

[18] *Hawthorn Report*, Vol. 1, pp. 114-116.

[19] Michael Harrington, *The Other America*, New York, Penguin Books, 1962, p. 156.

# 4
## Anomic Indians
## in the Native Social Structure

To this point the study has concerned itself with only two kinds of reserve families: the well-off and the dependent. It has been demonstrated that there is a very clear carry-over from these levels into the respective urban components of the Indian stratification system. The "leading families" (with their counterparts from other reserves and well-off Metis families) form the *Affluent*, while the "indigents" merge into a welfare "culture of poverty." On the one hand, a group of already well-acculturated families and individuals moves into positions of leadership in the urban areas; on the other, a large proportion of the Indian-Metis population, already maladjusted on the reserve, maintains its life-style in the city. In both cases, then, the change is predictable; migration does not decisively affect the character of the groups.

However, large numbers of Indians, individuals and families, lie socially between the *Affluent* and the *Welfare*, trying to adapt to the city, but without success. They do not have the psychological and social advantages of the *Affluent*; they are not technically as well-equipped, nor do they have the contacts required to deal effectively with white society; but they are unwilling to accept skid row. They are suspended between the city and the reserve.

The adjective "anomic" best describes their condition, for in the city they suffer personal disorientation, anxiety and social isolation of such magnitude that they either are forced down into the *Welfare* or return dejectedly to the reserve.[1] They aspire to preserve their Indian heritage and to adapt it to urban life – a posture of integration rather than assimilation. What is at stake is not "success in white terms" or "the internalization of the work norms of white society." The issue, rather, is personal control and participation, and an opportunity for creative activity in general. The minimal conditions are, first, the escape from bureaucratic control and welfare dependence, and, second, an urban milieu in which the Indian heritage can reinforce the pursuit of distinct cultural goals. But unlike the *Affluent* and *Welfare, Anomic* Indians do not have a reserve inheritance that equips them to reach their objectives. This can be demonstrated by studying their status on the reserve, prior to migrating to the city.

## The Anomic Migrants

Among the descendents of Victor Sunderland on the Swallow Lake Reserve, we have noted the two loose family groupings that can be discerned *between* the "leading families" on the one hand and the "confirmed indigent" on the other. The first of these was termed "self-supporting." To recapitulate, these families and individuals: 1) do not farm profitably, raise cattle or own modern machinery; 2) do not have incomes of over $3,000.00 per annum; 3) do not have prestigious connections with institutions of the larger society; but 4) have houses of five rooms or more.

During slack work periods, or during winter, the "self-supporting" families may apply for unemployment insurance and other benefits, but they are not directly dependent on welfare. Social assistance remains subordinate to income obtained from gainful employment. Although comprising only a small percentage of the total reserve population, this family grouping has generated a large number of migrants to urban areas.

The second source of *Anomic* Indian migrants, and the grouping immediately below the "self-supporting" but above the "confirmed indigent," has been termed "semi-dependent." The families and individuals in this category on the Swallow Lake Reserve are: 1) relatively poorer than the "self-supporting," with incomes of $2,000.00 per annum or less; 2) have small dilapidated houses, with few household conveniences; 3) do not own property of any value, and do not farm; and 4) typically have intermittent but severe family breakdowns.

The "semi-independent," may derive the bulk of their income from public assistance, but these families and individuals have not totally given up their struggle to escape welfare dependence through employment, or for their children, through education. They have not accepted slum life as the best alternative in a bitter world. There is, in short, a far greater potential for adjustment among reserve Indians than the stereotype would suggest. Our task now is to trace the fortunes in the city of those migrants who derive from the vulnerable, intermediate, reserve family groupings.

Unlike the *Welfare* and the *Affluent*, the *Anomic* Indians in the city lead so volatile and unpredictable an existence that definable social structures peculiar to this grouping have not developed. There is little or no interaction with families and individuals in a similar predicament; each family lives out its own struggle for survival by itself. Either it makes it into the ranks of the *Affluent* or it will gravitate towards skid row.

Consequently, family studies form the most acceptable method for describing the lot of the *Anomic* migrant. Migrants from the "self supporting" and "semi-dependent" reserve groupings encounter distinct sets of difficulties in urban society. Swallow Lake Reserve examples illustrate them in detail.[2]

1. Wilfrid Lang had to face the initial difficulty of illegitimacy. For this reason among others (both his mother and grandmother were hard workers), he was anxious to leave the reserve and find a good job in the city. Eventually he found his way to Saskatoon. For two years after 1966 he worked as a CNR timekeeper, quitting in August 1968 for a better position with the Canadian Agricultural Research Division at $1.92 per hour. By that time he and his common-law wife had a small child.

Unfortunately his change of job coincided with a slump in the economy. In January he was forced to approach the Indian Affairs Branch office for assistance with rent. After obtaining his new job, he had taken a new suite; it had been a costly move, and he needed $40 in order to cover the rent for the next month. Four months later he was laid off, with the possibility of being rehired in May. He told the IAB Placement Officer that he knew of an opening with the Department of Highways and thought that he could get it. In the interim his family required groceries. The Placement Officer authorized a $40 grant for groceries and advised him to stick with the Agricultural Research Laboratory.

Although he obtained the job with the Department of Highways, he was laid off again for two days at the end of May because of rain. He had not yet been paid, and needed further immediate assistance. Without savings, and with only a Grade XI education, in the vagaries of a bleak employment market, he experienced a continuing crisis situation during the entire next year. For several months things went all right, but he was laid off again in November and forced to come to the Indian Affairs Branch office for a subsidy. In January he required assistance for heating oil, and was advised to approach the Department of Social Welfare. According to the Placement Officer, he was having a "rough time."

The job situation, however, is only one side of the story. Considering his educational level, he had an excellent work record. In no instance had he left a job on his own initiative, except to obtain a better position. Moreover, until the spring of 1969, when the job situation became intolerable, he had not gone to the IAB for assistance – a rather impressive achievement when it is so easy to obtain short-term social benefits from a Placement Officer. Nevertheless, he was forced to obtain relief as soon as he was laid off, since saving of any kind was impossible in his home. Given the social position of the family on the reserve, members of the extended family were not inhibited about crashing, unconcerned about the enormous pressure on the home economy. At all times, the home was full of numerous relatives who came to live with the already hard-pressed family. It was not possible for him to turn them out, given their certain resentment of such unilateral action. Wilfrid would cut the last links with his family if he turned them away hungry.

Martha Lang, his mother, belongs to the "semi-dependent" grouping on the reserve. She and Wilfrid hover at the welfare line. He has accepted and internalized the success goals of the larger society, but his access to them is blocked. The larger society has been at least partially successful in inculcating in the family both a desire for, and a felt necessity to achieve, financial independence. But the reserve institutional system does not foster these aspirations – indeed, it works directly against them. The socialization process, combining elements of two diverse value systems, results in a "strain toward anomie."

Without the family disciplining of the "leading families," Wilfrid has nevertheless been led to believe that financial independence and work are worthwhile objectives. Unfortunately, he has limited realistic opportunities in the city. He must live in housing similar to that of the *Welfare* Indians and Metis; he has little chance for a steady job on the market, and does not have the reserve background required for an *Affluent* position. Like the other Indians in the city, his affiliation with the Church has collapsed, leaving reserve friends as his main social support.

Unfortunately, they devour his chances for success. The prime condition for anomic behaviour is fully realized: the "dissociation between culturally prescribed aspirations and socially structured avenues for realizing these aspirations."[3]

2. Harvey Lang, his cousin, three years younger and with a partial Grade XII education, has fared better. Unlike Wilfrid, Harvey was a legitimate child with a particularly ambitious mother, Jane Best, from Dakota Reserve. Both his parents emphasized education for their children and they were able to remain "self-supporting," independent of the welfare syndrome. However, they were by no means a "leading family." Joe Lang drove the school bus, generating a small but sufficient income which Jane handled very efficiently, but they did not farm, and were not socially prestigious on the reserve. The difference in family background between the two Lang boys was crucial. Whereas Wilfrid had a disadvantaged start, Harvey was raised in a stratum which unequivocally stressed the virtues of saving and education.

Nonetheless, the transition to the city was exceedingly difficult for Harvey. Since he did not belong to a "leading family," he was not automatically assured of a position of leadership in the urban environment. As an intelligent young Indian who had managed to win a special student award for Indians, he was caught up in an atmosphere of the Indian revival, but he did not have the necessary connections to take proper advantage of it. Had he finished Grade XII, he could have entered the university, with all the accompanying privileges for Indians. Had he had the proper connections, he could have worked for an Indian organization and rapidly attained a local reputation.

Instead, for two years he went from job to job throughout Saskatchewan (acquiring a wife and child on the way), looking for the executive-type position which he felt he merited. In the end he slipped into the ranks of the *Affluent,* but only through an unusually fortunate local contact. By that time, he had very nearly failed, and was at the point of dropping into the ranks of the native *lumpenproletariat.*

The story of his two years' struggle to escape dependence gives an interesting indication of the dilemma of native people who find themselves just below the *Affluent* level, but with similar ambitions and talents, and determined to rise to that level.

While still at school, Harvey had worked as a youth counsellor on the Swallow Lake Reserve. During the following year, he worked with a provincial study group, dealing with reserve housing problems. With these qualifications, he visited the Placement Officer in Saskatoon, and told him that he wanted to work with Indian people. He therefore sent applications to both the IAB and IMB.

Almost immediately, a position came open at an excellent retraining school and Indian Affairs Branch personnel in Saskatoon were anxious that Harvey take the job. A special trip was made by the Placement Officer to his reserve to inform him about the opening. According to the officer's report, he was broke, and a subsidy was necessary in order to get him to the city in time for an interview.

The interview was successful, and he was accepted as a supervisor. During all this time, the Indian Affairs Branch agreed to pay for his hotel accommodations and gas. Immediately after he accepted the position, application was submitted for a Manpower Grant to assist him and his family to move off the reserve. The total cost of relocation came to $705.20.

From the first, things did not go well at the School. As early as October, grocery assistance was requested in order to supplement a low salary. During the winter, he terminated employment, explaining to the Placement Officer that he thought he would get a better job in the administration of a far Northern reserve. In fact, he did not get the position.

During this period he was supported by the Department of Social Welfare in Saskatoon, where he now wished to settle. Harvey was advised by the IAB to go to several department stores to see about job openings; he replied that it was "too windy to try to find a job." "This chap," claimed the Placement Officer, "is very hard to understand."

In May 1968, he called the IAB to see if he could get summer work as a placement counsellor in Saskatoon. The Placement Officer remarked in his diary:

> ... didn't encourage because the past employment record does not enhance his qualifications for such employment. Doubt if this chap really knows what he wants to do – every time a suggestion is made he has some excuse or starts talking about some other job prospects – agree that his record was not enviable.

After two months of job-hunting, he did get a job as houseman at a small city hotel. The pay was miserable ($1.46 an hour) and he requested $125.00 assistance for rent, food, and clothes for the next month. Within two months he had quit, to the great annoyance of the hotel and the IAB office. There may have been other reasons for Harvey's departure from his job. Later in the month his aunt advised the IAB that he was ill and could not go to a hospital because he was not covered by medical insurance. He had been off reserve for longer than a year; his coverage had therefore expired. The Indian Affairs Branch office advised him that the Department of Social Welfare would pay all expenses if hospitalization should be necessary. He was immediately rushed to the hospital, where he spent over two weeks.

A week after leaving the hospital, Harvey Lang was again back at the IAB office, but now, apparently, he turned down all suggestions regarding employment. He saw no use in applying for a department store job because he felt he would be discriminated against. Further, he explained that the wage level was so low that he couldn't afford a baby sitter. The jobs offered simply did not meet his expectations. (He was for example, anxious for a job with a local radio station, but could not get it.)

It was urgent that the Department of Social Welfare increase its support if Harvey could not get a job. Yet there was less and less likelihood of this, for his record was becoming steadily bleaker, and his reputation was spreading around the province. The Indian Affairs Branch was fed up with him. It decided that he had had enough assistance, and refused to issue any further outlays. He was at the point of imminent decline.

At that moment he was saved by an official in the provincial Indian-Metis Branch in Saskatoon, who hired him to do a labour survey in the city. It was obviously the kind of job that appealed to him; it was prestigious, it concerned Indians, and it was a point of entry into the *Affluent*.

From this point on, he never looked back. After he had shown that he could get results, the Indian-Metis Branch hired him on a permanent basis. Having overcome the period of indecision, and having obtained an appropriate job, he had no difficulty in adapting to city life, stabilizing his family, and in finding very adequate housing in a better part of town. With a government job, he could now apply for, and obtain, off-reserve housing.

The problem of relatives, however, remained, although it had never been as severe as in the case of Wilfrid Lang. He was unusually fortunate in having an aunt in Saskatoon in the *Afflu-ent* class, with whom he spent a great deal of time. The connection both shielded him from dependents from his own reserve, and brought him into a home atmosphere which stressed work and habits of saving. Nonetheless, he felt it was necessary to have an unlisted phone number, and to guard carefully his exact address in the city.

Given the high rents in Saskatoon, Wilfrid was never able to escape from the poorer sections of the city; located on the West Side, he could hardly foil the determined searches of relatives. Fortunately for him, Harvey lived far away from the deep West Side.

3. Yet a third variant of the *Anomic* Indian is demonstrated by the case histories of two other families on a level below that of Wilfrid Lang, but still slightly above that of the families totally dependent on welfare on the reserve. The "indigents" Ralph Neville and Martin Neville have large families of seven and nine children respectively. Ralph's family was one of the poorest on the reserve; Martin was illegitimate, but his mother maintained a slightly more promising household. Martin had been a gas station attendant on the reserve, and had picked sugar beets in Alberta. Later that year he came to Saskatoon to do some construction work at $2.02 an hour. Ralph sought work that same year in the potash industry. Although he was mechanically gifted, it was decided that he was not well-trained enough to handle hydraulic machinery in the mines. He did get a job surfacing streets and promptly brought his family into Saskatoon, against the advice of the Indian Affairs Employment Officer. He then quit his job. Apparently he had been a good worker, for according to the Placement Officer, the employer was sorry to see him go and was willing to rehire him at any time. Martin Neville similarly quit his job by October and went back to the reserve; Ralph followed him. On January 10, the Indian Affairs Branch office in Saskatoon was presented with the light and power accounts which the families had left behind them; dutifully it paid the bills.

Martin stayed on the reserve for two years when Canada Manpower sponsored him for a carpentry course. Ralph, however, came to Saskatoon again almost immediately and once more began work surfacing streets. The main problem this time was apparently the difficulty of finding housing. The family had been one of the messiest on the reserve. Their own house and yard were littered with empty tin cans. On one occasion on the reserve, in the new house built for them by the IAB, Ralph and his wife took out an entire partition to increase the dancing area for a party. The wall was never replaced, leaving a jagged, nail-covered opening through the length of the house.

Landlords in Saskatoon did not take kindly to this rather laissez-faire attitude towards household cleanliness. While there, Ralph and his wife were constantly bombarded with complaints and forced to move with their seven children.

Martin's reappearance in Saskatoon seemed to mark a hopeful new departure. At least the Placement Officer was convinced that this time he would get a good job and stick with it. Martin was overheard to say that he definitely did not want to go back to the reserve, but rather wanted to become a prosperous carpenter. Interviews were arranged, and various companies expressed interest in hiring him. After finishing his course, however, he mysteriously disappeared. He and his family have recently turned up on the reserve, as have Ralph and his family after a stormy session in Saskatoon.

Both families appear condemned to a continual movement between the reserve and the city; both appear quite incapable of adjusting to the urban environment. In Martin's case, the difficulty has a great deal to do with the sheer anxiety of living in the city. Ralph, on the other hand, is more content to live in the urban *Welfare* class or as a total dependent on the reserve. Martin aspires to a relatively independent existence, but cannot break the stranglehold of the reserve. The only reason that Ralph even tries to take a job is to please his wife, for she is a granddaughter of Thomas McKnight and an ambitious woman.

Unlike Ralph, his wife Nora is interested in education and would have liked to become a school teacher. Unfortunately, Grade x will not do. She now takes revenge by tormenting upgrading teachers who visit the reserve. In contrast, Ralph has Grade iv, two of his siblings are retarded, and he has no interest in education whatsoever. Confronted by his wife, however, he is periodically lurched off the reserve and into jobs in the city.

Both Ralph and Martin were confronted by the problem of relatives when in Saskatoon; it was perhaps not decisive for Ralph, but may have been so for Martin. In neither case was there sufficient income for their own large families, much less a surplus to provide for visitors. Yet both are from families that take sharing customs for granted, and they can scarcely make enemies on the reserve while their position in the city is so tenuous.

## Discrimination and Abuse

No Indian in Canada can so much as walk down a street without being hurt – the stares, the cruel asides, the silences, the constant reminders that he is an outsider and a deviant. Wherever he goes, whatever he does, he can never escape the martyrdom of living in a hostile environment. It is not even absent from the closest relationships with white friends – a thousand words betray an ambiguity. The Indian withdraws in face of contrived sympathy, retreating into a different impenetrable world where he cannot be exploited. In their "friendships" with Indians in fact, whites are almost invariably self-serving in some way; usually, these days, they try to pry information out of the Indians. The embarrassed tatters of conversation mark the academic's need for data. In the end, the Indian who trusts a white intellectual will soon be disappointed, for, all promises notwithstanding, he will be abandoned and forgotten just as soon as the book is written.

Abuse of this kind is an objective feature of life in Canada, a permanent aspect of the social landscape in the larger society. But the groupings of Indians in the city react to it in different ways. The *Welfare* adjust by admitting defeat and rejecting the urban institutions which embody white values. By accepting the white stereotype of the "Indian," they gain a kind of freedom in skid row. Here there is enough community to prevent alienation. Meanwhile there is amusement in tricking white society out of minimal resources.

The *Affluent* have certain advantages in dealing with this form of social ostracism, and in any case, they are less vulnerable than the other groupings. For they have status and financial security; they have close relationships with other Indian families and usually a set of community institutions that provide a measure of satisfaction. That they are hurt by intended or unintended abuse goes without saying. The consequences are merely less severe.

The weapon of the *Affluent* is the ritualistic public denunciation of the Indian Affairs Branch and white society in general. Given its status, the Indian elite need not fear condemning real or imagined abuse. Indeed, as we shall see later, certain white groups not only condone criticism by native people, but foster it.

93

Whether speaking for themselves or in the name of native organizations, the *Affluent* can compensate somewhat for the pricks and needling of urban society.

The *Anomic* native people are exposed to the worst effects of abuse and discrimination, and have the least possibility of protecting themselves. Alone, isolated, and with fragile incomes and home economies, the potential for withstanding rejection is not high. The individual or family must somehow retain a sense of self-respect and inner strength in an environment of impending unemployment, Indian Affairs Branch officials, welfare officers, and humiliation. At the same time, since it must live in delapidated housing in (or near) slum areas, the atmosphere surrounding the family is hardly supportive. By definition, children must go to the worst schools, with the worst delinquency records. And constantly they see, know and meet native people on skid row.

Active discrimination complicates life yet further. Let us assume, for example, that an *Anomic* Indian finds employment, and is treated fairly on the job. He is almost certain to encounter discrimination at home. The reasons are clear: since he is poor, he must deal with slumlords, the used furniture and used car dealers and the maintenance men of slum dwellings – in short, the semi-criminal element of urban society. According to the best tradition of ethnic mobility these parasites of the poor are moving upward on the backs of the Indians and other helpless people.

A case in point is furniture. Because the *Anomic* Indian migrant cannot afford a new sofa, he buys one that is used. Noting a safe situation, the dealer delivers one with a broken support. The Indian family is faced with a dilemma. If they demand their money back, the store-owner will simply say that the family broke it, and that the matter is no longer any of his business. If the Indian is upset, let him see a lawyer. The result is that the Indian family keeps the sofa as it is, and in a few weeks, *all* the supports are gone. The social welfare worker then reports that the family is "irresponsible," prone to breaking furniture, and generally in need of counselling.

A similar situation holds for maintenance. Time and time again in a delapidated Indian apartment on the West Side, the plumbing breaks or there is an electrical failure. In the former case, in particular, it is essential that repairs be made immediately, or the dwelling soon becomes uninhabitable. Yet maintenance men, especially plumbers, find fixing poor houses a bad business risk. Moreover, they know that *Anomic* Indians are in no position to create a row, even if their few possessions are ruined. Invisibility is powerlessness. To the social worker or bureaucrat the family has simply been "irresponsible" and deserves a severe lecture. Faced by discrimination, the *Anomic* is helpless. As a transitional man, he can only *react*. and is at the mercy of Chance.

The *Affluent* native people are now in a position to obtain immediate publicity in a case of discrimination, with the result that merchants and repairmen are on their guard. Service is fast and adequate. To complain is to have power. The *Anomic* and *Welfare* groupings are not able to reach the broader public, and are far too vulnerable to want publicity in any case. The native people on skid row have long ceased to worry about discrimination because they have nothing to protect. But the *Anomic* Indians and Metis are pinned and mounted like butterflies.

## Ethnic Stratification in the City and the Dilemma of the Anomic

In the popular mind, human beings tend to be classified into social types, and they are approached or avoided on the basis of this classification. The white stereotype of the Indian is an exceedingly simple one. Either he is seen as lazy, shiftless, unable to stick to a job, stupid and immoral; or he is romanticized as a noble savage. In neither case can one detect a knowledge of possible complexities among the native people.

The crux of the native stratification system in the city involves the complex clash of the reserve kinship groupings with the established rankings of the larger society. The carry-over and transformation of the reserve kinship system can be visualized as a streamlining and hardening out of the major sub-groupings.[4]

One group, the *Affluent*, has been tremendously mobile in the last few years. The form of this mobility, however, and its significance for both the Indian-Metis urban sub-system and the larger society, depend on its contribution to a viable ethnic stratification system in general.[5] A sharp line divides white and Indian social systems in the city, a cleavage which is deeper than inter-native splits. All the Indian and Metis groupings stand outside white society but each is nevertheless associated with specific levels of the white class structure.

The *Affluent* Indians and Metis have reached the equivalent of a lower middle to upper middle class status, not through economic or educational achievement, but through Government promotion on the basis of ethnicity. To be sure, the selection was "earned" by their location and performance in the reserve kinship system. However, we have seen that the "leading families" were dependent on Church and State for the maintenance of their family ranking even on the reserve. The *Affluent* in the bureaucracies would suffer a drastic decline in status were they to lose favour with the Government agencies that appointed them. Their power ranking over the native population is entirely a product of their positions. Were they to leave the bureaucracies, their consumption level would be seriously affected.

They nonetheless must be considered in a class ranking with white counterparts, since their occupations involve them in constant association with white lower middle class officials. Rarely does it appear that the white officials accept the native people as equals and come to be on intimate terms with them. In the office as well as outside, the two ethnic groups go their own way. The fact of participation in lower middle class activities, however, entails recognition in the larger society as well. To have mail sent to a Government office places the *Affluent* Indian a cut above the working class. Similarly, the acquaintance of high Government officials entails status very much envied by white middle class counterparts in the Indian Affairs Branch office.

The very fact, however, that the *Affluent* position in the social hierarchy is obtained through connections rather than achievement compels its members to be very careful both in the nature of their opposition to the Government, and in the preservation of their positions vis-à-vis other Indians and Metis. A status position in the bureaucracy is an important prize, and available plums must be preserved for kinship members. Essentially, the *Affluent* form a closed status group.

The *Welfare* Indians and Metis on the other hand form a vast extension of the white disreputable poor, based on the provision of welfare services from the larger community. The term "disreputable," however, should be restricted to the white class system, where rejects are castigated as being a wasteful excrescence. In terms of the Indian and Metis stratification system, the *Welfare* may very well be the most "normal" of the individual groupings.

Unlike both the *Affluent*, who have been propelled into a high status position, and the *Welfare*, who maintain an identity in the "culture of poverty," the *Anomic* are marginal in both native and white stratification systems. The *Anomic*, like the *Affluent*, aspire to a lower middle class status, but in the native social system they are *déclassés*, suspended between two stable status formations. They are isolated within their social system by virtue of their background in the kinship system, and they do not have the tools with which to compete successfully in the larger society. Thus the families and individuals who do try to survive in the urban environment are not protected from the superior competitive power of the society they are trying to enter. They lie scattered along the boundaries of the white working class. If the marginal man concept has any meaning at all, it refers to the invidious position of the *Anomic* in the urban environment.

---

[1] The terms "Anomie" and "Alienation" raise extremely important questions of definition and, therefore, ideological content. Contemporary American Social Science has gravely undermined the classical meanings of both concepts as set forth by Durkheim and Marx. "Not only is the role of values overlooked, but, under the guise of value-free sociology, the values are generally changed in a conservative direction." (J. Horton, "Dehumanization of Anomie and Alienation," in *British Journal of Sociology*, Vol. 15, Routledge and Kegan Paul, London, 1964, pp. 203-301.)

The cultural values of the dominant class, status and success, are accepted, rather than subjected to critical examination. The present study attempts not only to point out socio-economic barriers to the achievement of success, but also to reassert the radical content of these terms. (See also A. Dawe, "The Two Sociologies," in *British Journal of Sociology*, Vol. 21, 1970).

[2] Unless otherwise indicated, the case-studies are based on extensive interviews conducted in 1969-70, and on IAB *Placement Officer Reports*, Saskatoon, Saskatchewan.

[3] R. Merton, "Social Structure and Anomie," *Varieties of Modern Social Theory*, Hendrick M. Ruitenbuk, ed., New York, E. P. Dutton, 1963, p. 363; in *The Sioux Indian Student: A Study of Scholastic Failure and Personality*, Dr. John F. Bryde contends that the prolonged exposure of the Indian to two conflicting cultures under present circumstances results in normlessness and alienation – from himself, from his people, and from the larger society. The resultant feelings may be rejection, depression, or anxiety; H. B. Hawthorn, *op. cit.* pp. 323-324, similarly finds deviance to result from unfulfilled attempts at acculturation and assimilation. We agree with the trend of these findings, but limit their applicability to one stratum of urban Indians.

[4] According to one author:
"An essential characteristic of all known kinship systems is that they function as transmitters of inequalities from generation to generation. Similarly, an essential characteristic of all known stratification systems is that they employ the kinship system as their agent of transmitting inequalities." (Malvin N. Tumin, "Reply to Kingsley Davis," *Class, Status and Power*, R. Bendix and S. M. Lipset, eds., New York, Macmillan, 1966.)

[5] Several authors have noted that many dimensions are involved in a stratification system. Lipset has suggested the use of four: occupational rankings; consumption rankings; social class; and power rankings. In a racial society like the Cana-

dian, the presence of an unassimilable outside group introduces a whole new spectrum in conceptualizing vertical mobility. The successful destruction of the indigenous world in the European Conquest, and the demoralization and corruption of the native culture has meant that the reference group used by the native population in assessing its position in the larger society will be drawn from white society. To this extent acculturation is a fact. But the existence of an outside reference group does not imply value assimilation. Within the urban framework the division between the native and white populations shows no evidence of diminishing. As on the reserves, so also in the cities, Indians and Metis are now redefining the whole network of ties that exist between culturally autonomous native and white subsystems.

In short, acculturation can also be (and is better) perceived as an adaptation of the entire sub-system to new conditions, rather than as a continuum on which individuals of a non-westernized group move overwhelmingly away from traditionalism and towards westernization. According to Van Den Berghe, the colonial situation creates a "pluralist" society, to be distinguished from the loose term used by American political scientists to refer to partly overlapping political interest groups:

A society is pluralistic to the extent that it is structurally segmented and culturally diverse. In operational terms, pluralism is characterized by the relative absence of value consensus; the relative rigidity and clarity of group definitions; the relative presence of conflict, or, at least, a lack of integration and complementarity between the various parts of the social system; the segmentarian and specific character of the relationships, and the relative existence of sheer institutional duplication (as opposed to functional differentiations, specialization) between the various segments of a society. . . . In other words, a society is pluralistic insofar as it is compartmentalized into quasi-independent sub-systems, each of which has a set of institutions, and lays specific points of contact with others.

In the urban environment in Canada, the interaction between the two cultures appears to be based on toleration (or hostility) rather than consensus.

See also P. Van Den Berghe, "Sociology of Africa," *Africa: Social Problems of Change and Conflict*, ed., P. Van Den Berghe, San Francisco, Chandler Publishing Co., 1965, p. 78. Van Den Berghe cites interesting examples of program malintegration and even disintegration (South Africa, for example) which are embarrassingly relevant to the Canadian case. See also M. G. Smith, "Social and Cultural Pluralism," in *Africa: Social Problems of Change and Conflict, op. cit.,* p. 69.

# 5
## Urban Poverty Programs

New agencies at the federal, provincial and municipal levels of government have proliferated in the last decade. But the shadow of dependence on bureaucracies spreads over the Indian as he moves from the reserve to the city. Although some may question both the validity of the new programs and the sincerity of Government administrators, no one can deny the extraordinary expansion of services that has occurred in the whole area of Indian-Metis affairs. They take root with a purpose; they spread happily like ivy; their vines intertwine; the knots and tangles become ugly and dangerous; eventually their survival is their rationale. Indians are caught within this jungle, and must somehow cope with it.

### City Council
With one exception, the Indian and Metis Friendship Centre, the City of Saskatoon does not fund services directed exclusively at Indians and Metis. City Council does not appear to be unduly worried about the possible problems resulting from the migration of Indians and Metis to Saskatoon.

Businessmen report that they have an increasing number of Indian customers, and seem in general to be pleased by the arrival of this new and growing clientele. The Mayor and his aldermen believe that rapid growth in the city's native population is taking place, but they do not know where or how the native people live. According to one alderman, there is little or no communication between City Hall and the provincial and federal agencies dealing with Indians and Metis.

A few years ago, one of the more socially-conscious aldermen was instrumental in initiating a clean-up program to rid the West

Side (his own business area) of certain 'undesirable elements.' This area, around 20th Street West from Avenue A to Avenue F, as we have seen, is noted for a high incidence of prostitution and alcoholism, and is also the area where one sees the most Indians. The measure, principally a police operation, was fairly successful, and the matter of Indians was dropped thereafter. It has not reappeared at City Hall. In short, the 'Indian problem' at that time was considered part and parcel of the problem of lesser crime of the area.

All indications suggest that the city will give lip service to the need for improvement in the situation of native people living in Saskatoon, but will not raise its hand to initiate long-term projects or programs. Basically, the city's attitude is that Indians are none of its business, and that individual problems should be turned over to the IAB, the Indian-Metis Branch (provincial Government) the Department of Social Welfare or, in case of trouble, the police. It will only change its attitude if and when major trouble breaks out – when it will be too late.

For its part, the police department is indeed concerned about the increasing numbers of Indians and Metis in Saskatoon, and the greater incidence of petty crime involving them. According to the Deputy Police Chief, "there are just too darn many Indians in trouble these days." He pointed out that few of the incidents involved serious matters such as breaking and entering or criminal assault. The vast majority of charges had to do with alcohol, petty theft (in order to buy more liquor), disturbance of the peace and vagrancy.

The police have an added reason to be concerned. With the growth of Indian consciousness, they have been widely criticized for their treatment of Indians in custody or under arrest. Since a few charges of police violence have been substantiated, they are now anxious to prove that they do not discriminate against the native population.[1] The Deputy Police Chief expressed concern that the city was not engaged in long-term planning to meet the problems arising from a racial slum, and made reference to the experience of Winnipeg. He maintained close relations with the Salvation Army, the agency which he felt was in closest touch with the native population. Each day a Salvation Army officer drops by the Police Station to discuss the events of the previous night.

The police department is unquestionably in a difficult situation. The city refuses to accept responsibility for the Indians and

Metis, preferring to send them to the Government agencies that deal specifically with Indian and Metis affairs. Consequently, the burden of day-to-day business falls on the police. So far no major violence has erupted, but the police department must accept the onus of clearing the streets of petty crime.

## Federal and Provincial Programs

At the federal and provincial levels of Government, there are specialized agencies specifically designed to promote the successful urbanization of the native population. These operate alongside the services made available to all citizens of Canada, in particular those dealing with health, education and welfare.

**Graph 1**
**Growth of the Department of Indian Affairs and Northern Development (1958-1968)**

Source: Canada Department of Indian Affairs and Northern Development, Indian Affairs Branch, Annual Report 1969.

## The IAB

The Department of Indian Affairs entered the urban arena in 1957 when it launched its placement program; at first it was on an experimental basis, with offices in Toronto, Vancouver, Winnipeg and Edmonton. In 1959, Saskatoon also received a placement officer. The *Annual Report* of the Minister of Citizenship and Immigration for that year reveals a great enthusiasm for the new program:

101

During the first two years, when the operation was developing on an experimental basis, 295 young Indians entered the placement program. Of these only 32 were unable to settle into *permanent* jobs. In the first eight months of this year a further 169 entered the program and as of August 30, 133 were in permanent positions. Fifteen went back to their reserves; the remaining 21 were still in training.[2]

In the Minister's opinion, the program was designed for young people only; "careful selection" was therefore essential. Good education on the reserves was also stressed, for these Indians were meant to take *permanent* positions off the reserves. A high school diploma was considered advisable preparatory to learning new skills in the city.

The emphasis has been on quality rather than quantity. These young Indians are carefully selected at the high school level and must have a strong desire to work off the reserve in large urban centres. . . . These young people have a double hurdle to jump; not only must they adjust from a rural to an urban life, like many other young Canadians, but they must, having been brought up in one culture, adapt themselves to another.[3]

The placement program, then, was *not* designed for the seasonal migrant, for those with ties to the reserves, or for older people with family responsibilities. The Indians involved were to be the young elite, the small minority that had obtained a high school education.[4]

An integral part of the placement program was counselling to help young Indians cope with day-to-day problems of adjustment. Placement officers, therefore, had a double task: they had to select Indians and find suitable employment for them "in factories, offices, garages, stores"; and also to ensure that the relocatees were not overwhelmed in the process of transition.[5]

Internal momentum, the growing urgency of the problem, and increased provincial interest have resulted in a very significant change of approach in the IAB. Whereas in the early years, it was very concerned about the most careful selection of qualified relocatees, it now emphasizes *quantity* rather than *quality*. The priorities have been reversed since 1960. In addition, the IAB has gone beyond the goal of individual placement to assisting in family relocation. The "twenty families project" envisioned the successful relocation of twenty Indian families to the major Canadian urban centres, including Saskatoon. As these changes were taking place, the existing adaptive services were expanded in the fields of education, training programs and housing.

The pivotal importance of the IAB in Saskatoon demands a close look at the present range of its assistance. The IAB *Employment and Relocation* manual provides the following guidelines:

In respect of each individual included in the placement program:

1) Transportation from the Indian community to the place of employment and required food and accommodation en route, and, in the event of the failure of the individual to adjust, return transportation and required food and accommodation en route.

2) At the prevailing rate in the area, normally for a period up to two months: a) room and board, b) room, services and food. *But in neither case* beyond the time that the individual has established eligibility for provincial or municipal assistance.

3) Personal allowance not in excess of $25.00 per month, normally for a period up to two months and not beyond the time that the individual has established eligibility for provincial or municipal assistance.

4) Tools not in excess normally of $150.00.

5) Clothing not in excess of $100.00

6) On-the-job training contracts with employers on behalf of the individual, during a period of normally six months but not in excess of one year, these contracts to include where necessary the payment of a share of the individual's salary.[6]

Families receive additional benefits, which are not to total more than $3,000. These include: transportation; on-the-job training contracts for all members of the family; food; rent for apartments and houses; clothing; services such as electric power, fuel and other utilities; and household effects, the value to range between $700 and $1,000. Even for seasonal or short-term employees, the benefits to be obtained are quite considerable. Again from the Placement Officer's manual:

1) Transportation, food and lodging en route when necessary.

2) Work clothing when necessary, normally amounting to $50.00 or less.

3) Food supplies and tenting equipment, when necessary, pending receipt of earnings.

4) Tools in special circumstances when required to effect placement.

5) On-the-job training costs for periods up to six months with the Branch contributing up to 50 per cent of the trainee's wages during the period of the contract. e.g., provision of on-the-job training for an Indian boy in operating heavy equipment.[7]

Relocation grants offer a special incentive to Indian individuals and nuclear families who wish to leave the reserve. According to the employment manual, the IAB commits itself:

> . . . to provide financial assistance by ways of grants to Indian *individuals* and *families* to facilitate their permanent relocation from reserves to areas offering employment opportunity. This authority, which has now been decentralized to the Indian Commissioner and Regional Directors, provides for assistance up to a maximum of $5,000.00 to an individual or family to aid in the following: transportation; purchase of household effects; maintenance at prevailing rates; personal allowances as required; tools as necessary to facilitate placement in regular employment.[8]

As of August 1969, thirty-six relocation grants had been received by Indians to move to Saskatoon, but the average grant per family was less than $1,000. A figure lower than the maximum is entirely justified by instructions which state that "in situations where the Indian worker is in a position to assume some responsibility in the purchase of household effects or tools, the Branch should contribute to only a portion of the cost."[9]

The official manual places great stress on the integration of employment and relocation activity within the vocational, apprenticeship, training and "special services" function.[10] These latter are made available in provincial institutions (although directed and funded by the IAB); the Canada Manpower Service courses; or the regular Federal-Provincial Training Schools.

On-the-job trainees are urged to enter the provincial apprenticeship program which provides training in Saskatoon or Moose Jaw during the slack period in winter when they will probably be laid off. During these six to eight week courses, the apprentice is paid a living allowance and his tuition is waived. The hope is that after three or four years a candidate can qualify as a journeyman. An in-service training program is available for young people who have completed business or commercial courses, but who need office training. These are placed as trainees in federal or provincial government offices, or with an approved firm for a period not to exceed three months. The IAB will pay such a trainee $40.00 a week for that time, and of course assist in getting him permanent placement afterwards.

In the case of training programs as well, the various provincial and federal government agencies are expected to work together. In Saskatoon, their cooperation appears to be satisfactory, with the IAB, Manpower and the IMB all referring and nominating native people to courses available in the city – particularly in the sprawling Saskatchewan Institute for Applied Arts and Sciences.

*Present Policy and Scope*

Since 1967, the Indian Affairs Branch has administered an important housing program. The legislation which introduced the program merits a close reading. According to the then Indian Affairs Minister, Arthur Laing, it was designed "to ease the transition from the reserve to the materialistic urban society."[11] According to the regulations:

Indians and Eskimos who are regularly employed off reserves and who can give reasonable assurance that such employment is of a continuing nature may be assisted in obtaining off-reserve accommodation. In addition to regular employment, this program involves: 1) the credit and responsibility record of the applicant, 2) a personal contribution, based upon income, must be paid when application is made, by bank draft or money order or by certified cheque, payable to the Receiver General of Canada, 3) a repayable first mortgage to Central Mortgage and Housing Corporation or an approved lender (maximum related to applicant's income and ability to repay), 4) a second mortgage to a maximum of $10,000.00.[12]

What the program amounts to is a large conditional grant with a maximum amount of $10,000, linked to family income and the ability of the family to meet mortgage payments over and above the conditional grant.

"Conditional" refers to good behaviour. If the Indian or Eskimo family lives in the house for a period of ten years, the mortgage held by the Indian Affairs Branch will be erased. In order to ensure that the standards of the *National Housing Act* are not violated, two other federal agencies, the Veterans Land Administration and the Central Mortgage and Housing Corporation, must approve the house or the plans in the event of building. The off-reserve housing grant is an extraordinary benefit for those Indians and Metis with the necessary qualifications. Of all the programs, this is the most sought after; it is also by far and away the most difficult to obtain.

The basic philosophy of the IAB placement program with the related services is assimilation. It demands that Indians give up their heritage. Modelled on the relocation program of the Bureau of Indian Affairs in the United States, the Canadian placement program envisions adoptable Indian families and individuals living apart from one another, to preclude the formation of a ghetto.[13] In Winnipeg, even the idea of a "half-way-house" where Indians could stay until they had found permanent residence was rejected on the grounds that any native enclave must necessarily be pathological. Unlike the Voluntary Relocation Program in the United States in its earlier years, the IAB has been more restrained in pursuing assimilation in the urban environment. According to one Minister, the Indians need time, "to adjust to the jet-paced world of modern technology," although she was in no doubt about the end product. "[Assimilation] . . . cannot be prevented. The more realistic question is: 'How soon, and by what means?'"[14]

## Provincial Programs

The IAB relocation program has in recent years been joined by the massive extension of provincial Indian and Metis services. In Saskatchewan, in fact, provincial interest has provided a major stimulus for this increased service to the native population. According to the late Premier Ross Thatcher, the Indian-Metis

106

problem is "a time bomb ... Saskatchewan's number one social problem." Immediate action is required to overcome "an almost insurmountable problem of explosive proportions."[15] A special Indian-Metis Branch in the Department of Natural Resources was set up by the Premier in 1965; in 1969, as previously indicated, it was raised to the status of a Department of Indian and Metis Affairs.

To assist the new Department, a Saskatchewan Task Force on Indian Opportunity was set up to enquire into problems of education, training, housing and employment. Represented on the Task Force are business, industry, mining, the University of Saskatchewan, the teaching profession, cooperatives, labour, the churches, representatives of the Indians and Metis, the three levels of Government and the Saskatchewan Legislature.

The stated objectives of the Indian-Metis Department do not differ in any fundamental way from those of the IAB in regard to urban programs, although it does include the Metis within its jurisdiction. Employment relocation is the fundamental method used to reduce native dependence on welfare.[16] Indeed, Thatcher has repeatedly stated that employable Indians and Metis will not obtain social aid: "We do not believe that the State owes anyone a living if that individual is too lazy to work."[17] During the summer and autumn months of 1968, drastic cuts were made in welfare payments to "able-bodied Indians and Metis as an incentive to work."[18]

As in the case of the IAB, the new Indian-Metis Department emphasizes educational up-grading and training, and has counselling services to assist relocatees. Provincial placement officers are instructed to work with the federal Department of Indian Affairs, with Manpower, (which has no fewer than three offices in Saskatoon) and others, to persuade natives to leave the reserves and to take employment.

Placement and counselling services are open to all who come to the offices, providing there is staff available to see them. Unlike the Indian Affairs Branch, which is authorized to assist only the registered Indians (although the occasional non-treaty Indian or Metis finds his way into the Branch office), the provincial Government has jurisdiction over Metis and non-registered Indians. If placement is obtained by the Indian-Metis applicant, that is, if it can be shown that he will be staying in the city on a job for at least some time and an opening is found, he is eligible for a variety of additional supports to "help him along."

If the job applicant is quite promising, a full month's rent is provided along with clothing and food allowances, *plus* assistance in bringing furniture from the North or off the reserve. Slightly less suitable migrants do not get the furniture money, but obtain all the other benefits, estimated at roughly $215.00 for parents with one or two dependents. The off-reserve housing program of the provincial Government is similarly operational. Its plan is to buy old houses in cities, in cooperation with municipal authorities, and to make them available to suitably qualified Indians and Metis.[19] These are principally veterans' homes, customarily referred to as wartime shacks, built after the Second World War. Most of these houses are in clusters and are not in prime residential areas. A concentration of veterans' houses in Saskatoon implies decline in the neighbourhood. However, the homes must pass inspection by the Central Mortgage and Housing Corporation before they can be inhabited by Indians and Metis. Therefore at least when the family enters the home, there is some guarantee of minimal standards. As of 1969 11 houses had been purchased in the Saskatoon area by the provincial government and the IMB office was busy searching for relatively well adapted, or "adaptable" Indians and Metis to live in them. The Indian-Metis Branch works closely with the provincial Department of Social Welfare, conveniently located in the adjacent building. But in practice access to this welfare assistance is more difficult for native people than for non-Indians.

Although in theory anyone from anywhere in Canada can enter a provincial Social Welfare office, obtain a form, and expect a decision based on an objective assessment of need and similar qualifications, Indians in practice are referred to the IMB or IAB office to consult a counsellor or to find a job. The decision about welfare is made by the official, who can either provide the Indian in question with room and board for a "trial" period, or send him back to the reserve, or recommend assistance by the Department of Social Welfare. In any case, the Indian is at a considerable disadvantage – special status limits his chances of participating in the most effective social assistance program in the province.

**The Programs Compared**

In the field of urban relocation in Saskatoon, the federal Government remains paramount. While the Indian Affairs Branch placed 1277 men and women in regular and short-term employment, the local provincial office accounted for only 302 placements in the same period.[20]

The difference in importance is reflected in the dimension of respective offices. From a staff of two in 1960, the IAB in 1972 has twenty-four administrators in the city along with supportive staff. The Indian-Metis Branch, on the other hand, while expanding rapidly, has as yet a much smaller staff – four full-time officers and secretaries. In placement, education and housing programs, the province lags far behind the IAB.

Indians and Metis need not wait for referral by the IAB or the IMB; they can bypass these agencies, going directly to Manpower. However, few Indians appear to ignore the IAB if they are interested in employment. IAB and IMB officials have estimated that 90 per cent of Indians seeking jobs use their services.

The unwritten belief among government administrators is that all the programs taken together will foster self-help and better work habits among the Indians and Metis of Saskatchewan. It is admitted that many native people do not keep their jobs. It is also admitted that the problem of adjusting to white society will be great. But the two major agencies, along with the Department of Social Welfare, agree that the carrot of better living conditions derived from gainful employment, and the stick of the threat of losing welfare money, will lead the native people to accept the values of the larger society regarding personal discipline and work. "Institution-building" of this kind will narrow the gap between the Indians and Metis and the white society. Moreover, the spread effect will be rapid, given economic and social development programs on the reserves and in the North. The cities will find themselves with an increasingly active, skilled, and acculturated minority.[21]

Essentially the "spread effect" strategy is an adaptation of the "self-support" philosophy on the reserves. In both cases, assimilation is the goal. The former strategy tries to force the Indians and Metis to reform themselves in urban areas outside the reserves, while the proponents of "self-support" want to accomplish the job on the reserves *before* the natives reach the towns and cities.

**Voluntary Programs**

The belief in Canada that private charity is more morally uplifting than government services dies hard. To be good is to give; to give is to make a donation of time or money to a specific

109

worthy cause: ladling soup into outstretched bowls; campaigning for the Heart Fund; collecting for the Missions. Government programs, on the other hand, are morally neutral, regrettable concessions to the brute fact that parish relief and charitable contributions in general no longer meet the poverty question in an advanced industrial state.

Voluntary programs nonetheless play an important role in the welfare field. Many are not very conspicuous and many are small. The point is that there are *many*, more or less well-funded, from United Appeal, churches, private subscriptions or even government authorities. Taken together, the voluntary programs form a backstop for the larger official welfare agencies. Is not the worthiest cause the most destitute in society, the most derelict? Essentially the churches and charitable groups paper over cracks in the world of urban welfare.

That the Indian cause should attract the attention of charitable groups goes without saying. What a splendid opportunity, given the long association with churches on the reserves and all. In Saskatoon, for example, in recent years the network of voluntary organizations in the welfare field has been redirecting efforts towards the native community as it has grown. Catholic Family Services, supported largely by the United Appeal, has an active case list of some eighty families. The Family Services Bureau, unofficially Protestant, similarly champions the native cause. The Salvation Army operates a large hostel, a Social Service Centre, a Suicide Prevention Bureau, Family Thrift Stores, a Senior Citizens' Home, the Bethany House and Hospital, a youth camp, a Correctional Services Bureau and a Family Services office. Alcoholics Anonymous has a large Indian clientele in Saskatoon. And so on.

The work of two of these voluntary programs will be assessed here to illustrate the impact of charity on the lives of destitute Indians and Metis in Saskatoon. Without them, survival on Skid Row would be far more difficult.

## The Salvation Army

The Salvation Army has been for ever and for all places described by George Orwell.[22] On 19th Street and Avenue C in Saskatoon, in the heart of the West Side, a block away from two major and notorious bars, and a half-block from a house of dubious reputation, lies the same massive rejection of anything beautiful and dignified. The visitor is confronted by omnipresent disinfectant; dusty plastic curtains; a sustained and militant ignorance; an urgency of the apocalypse; and around the halls, in the office, the TV room and the chapel, a sense of impending masturbation. Everywhere there is nothingness. Even the file cabinets are creaking and rusty. Behind a wired opening, the custodians interview and lecture the clientele in the most personal terms and always in double negatives. If accepted, or indeed if rejected, the client shuffles into the TV room or loiters around the hallway, drifting periodically into the friendly neighbourhood Thrift Store to see what is available on that front.[23]

Situated in a prairie city on the trans-continental route, the Salvation Army of Saskatoon receives an unusually large number of single male human wrecks, drifting from one city to the next. The common characteristic of the Salvation Army as a haven for social rejects is amply substantiated by extensive contact with that institution. Life in the Salvation Army symbolizes failure in the larger society; it is a depressed, although not necessarily brutal, home for male outsiders.

The Indians and Metis who visit the Salvation Army do not entirely fit this stereotype, a fact which becomes apparent after many afternoons of observation. Despite a high number of dilapidated native people who seek refuge for the night, many young Indians and Metis use the Salvation Army as a hotel rather than a flop house.[24] Among the native people in general, with the exception of the *Affluent*, there appears to be none of the social stigma attached to the Salvation Army that there is in white society. The *Affluent* have not visited the Salvation Army, either before or after coming to the city. Thus it provides another indication of the social distance between the top stratum of the native urban minority and the other groupings.

While the *Affluent* have internalized white middle class norms, the other Indians use the Salvation Army hostel because it is free and because meal tickets can be obtained. In discussion, Indians depict the Salvation Army as just another form of welfare available to the public. Since native people are used to welfare, no great significance is attached to the special flavour of the institution.[25] One young Indian who used the Salvation Army regularly, staying there for three days each month, and either staying with relatives and friends or going back to the reserve between visits, commented that:

> I like visiting the city. There is more to do here than on the reserve. It sure is lucky that there is a place to stay when one

comes in and I sure feel sorry for those Indians who don't know about the Salvation Army. The lucky ones know about it and can stay here for three days. That's a big help. Sometimes one can find some work in three days or sometimes one can meet friends to stay with; the Salvation Army doesn't tie one down.

The importance of the Salvation Army to transient and resident Indians and Metis in Saskatoon can scarcely be overestimated; its records are an indispensable source of information for the researcher and planner. Over the last ten-year period, 26.1 per cent of the total number of visitors were native people; in the last three years, the Salvationists estimate that roughly 50 per cent of the clientele has been Indian and Metis.[26] The annual increase is marked. Between 1958 and 1968 total visits of native people to the Salvation Army hostel increased from 5 to 1800 annually.

A significant change in the number of visits by month occurred between 1965 and 1968. In 1968, the monthly fluctuations appear more closely geared to the employment situation. The peak month for 1965 is July, the month of the Saskatoon Exhibition, which was (and is) an event of some popularity that might be expected to draw Indians in from the reserves. In contrast, the peak months in 1968 are May and September, when seasonal jobs are beginning and ending. Indeed, in the fiscal year 1967-1968, 684 Indian people sought jobs, of whom 564 or 82.5 per cent were male, qualifying for Salvation Army assistance. No fewer than 186, or 33 per cent, stayed at the Salvation Army at the time of application; 378, or 67 per cent, were residents there at one time or another.

Certainly the evidence from the Salvation Army alone gives a preliminary indication of growth of migration and employment interest. But the Salvation Army records also indicate the origin of the bulk of the clients, and therefore give a clue as to the effect of geographical barriers on the population movement. Some 88.8 per cent of the natives had Saskatchewan addresses. Particularly striking is the number of people from the Northern agencies who did not obtain employment. The employment records of the IAB for 1967-1969, for example, show that only 46 people from the Meadow Lake agency in the far North were placed, although no fewer than 240 were registered at the Salvation Army.

The posture adopted by the Salvationist attendant toward the

Indian and Metis is one of unrelenting paternalism mingled with contempt. They are viewed as foreigners as a matter of course. A ritual is involved when an Indian comes in to find a bed for the night. First, the custodian will severely lecture the fellow about the importance of working. Then he will privately express his belief that the native population is incapable of meeting the responsibilities of family and city life. Salvationists do express concern at the growing number of native people who are using the Salvation Army, but not without a glow in the eye which emphasizes a new role for the Salvation Army itself, for the Indians and Metis in the city represent an incomparable religious challenge. Given the decline of traditional Christian beliefs among the native people, the Salvationists are by no means unhappy about the large numbers flocking to their hostel and other services in the city.

The disturbing thing, however, is that employable Indians and Metis who use the Salvation Army as a more or less regular base in the city are extremely badly placed for entrance into good jobs or responsible positions. Close observation suggests that many of the Indians who come to the hostel simply have no other place to go in the city. They are potentially able and willing to accept employment responsibilities, but living at the Salvation Army renders them social outcasts in the eyes of the larger society.

The Salvationists are one of the few groups in the city that give more than lip-service to assistance for the native population, that investigate charges of discrimination, and that care for the sick and the aged. It is also true that they have a vested interest in retaining the Indian-Metis as a religious clientele group, preferably homogenized, with whom religious righteousness can be exercised. There is absolutely no indication that the Salvation Army views the present condition of the native people against an enlightened historical background. Indians and Metis are poverty-stricken because they are wicked or lazy, and probably both. Indians and Metis who frequent the Salvation Army are aware of this attitude, but such similar views are evident in the Indian Affairs Branch, the Indian-Metis Branch and places of employment and entertainment, that so slight an indignity can be tolerated for a free service. However, by frequenting the Salvation Army, the Indians and Metis remove themselves still further from the larger society; the Salvation Army casts its ideology of dereliction and hopelessness over the Indian and Metis sub-culture in the city.

## The Friendship Inn

Another church-supported agency in Saskatoon has had a major impact on the native minority in the city. The Friendship Inn, located on 20th Street and Avenue E – on the West Side like the Salvation Army – is not operated exclusively for Indians and Metis, but about 50 per cent of its visitors are natives, the largest single clientele group.

Conceived of as a Marian Centre by the Roman Catholics, the Friendship Inn became an inter-denominational project of the Inter-City Council of Churches. Each week one of the fifty-two parishes in the community gathers sufficient food and volunteer help to serve about 600 meals to the city poor. Two women from the Social Planning Council are on hand for free counselling. A clothing bank and barber's chair are available, and third-year law students operate a free legal-aid clinic in non-criminal matters. More than three years after its official opening in March 1969, the Friendship Inn is still a roaring success. According to its Director, the Department of Social Welfare has been so impressed by the turnout that it is prepared to finance a "serenity farm" where people could dry out while hoeing potatoes for their daily meals. The Inn is working with Alcoholics Anonymous, the Bureau of Alcoholism and the Department of Social Welfare to "get them off skid row."

Given the numbers involved, the connection with the Indian problem is obvious. The Director as well as two sets of volunteers explicitly indicated that this was their central concern. Only Indians who have not been drinking, "who have no vanilla extract [and ] I know where the bulges are," can get their meal. For those who qualify under these rules, the food is excellent, and they may eat as much as they can devour (with a pinched bun or two on the side). The Friendship Inn represents an extraordinary source of sustenance. In conjunction with the Salvation Army, the Indian-Metis Friendship Centre, the IAB, the IMB, the Department of Social Welfare, the Family Agencies, and smaller welfare agencies, it is an invaluable dietary oasis for the indigenous population on the West Side.[28]

## Conclusion

The extension of services to urban Indians and Metis is an

undeniable fact. Urban poverty programs now form a very significant part of Indian Affairs expenditures. There is no question that these services are now significant enough to induce Indians and Metis to leave their communities and migrate to the cities. Even the voluntary programs can keep some one going for a few days while he looks around. The effect on the native community in the city, however, deserves careful study.

---

[1] *Saskatoon Star-Phoenix*, March 22, 1969; April 1, 1969.

[2] Fairclough, "Indian Affairs in 1959," *op. cit.*, p. 50.

[3] *Idem.*

[4] The IAB at the same time stressed the importance of Indians obtaining jobs whenever industry moves into areas in which Indians are living – a reference to primary industries such as logging, pulp cutting, road clearing and mining. For example, "northern employers have found Indians particularly well-adapted to outdoor work." *Idem.*

[5] Fairclough, "Indian Affairs in 1960," *op. cit.*, p. 38.

[6] Department of Citizenship and Immigration, Indian Affairs Branch, *Employment and Relocation Programs, op. cit.*, pp. 20-21.

[7] *Idem.*

[8] *Idem.*

[9] Department of Citizenship and Immigration, Indian Affairs Branch, *Employment and Relocation Manual, op. cit.*, p. 6.

[10] "Special services" refers to Canada Manpower Service programs, including the "Selected Young Indian Program," the "Manpower Mobility Program," and a variety of other federal auxiliary services. See *Ibid.*, pp. 6-10.

[11] *The Indian News*, December, 1967.

[12] Department of Indian Affairs and Northern Development, *Indian Off-Reserve and Eskimo Re-establishment Regulations*, Ottawa, p. 1.

[13] Compare J. Ablon, "Relocated Indians in the San Francisco Bay Area," *op. cit.*, p. 298. "The stated Bureau housing policy is to disperse the general population to further the goal of assimilation."

[14] Ellen Fairclough, "Indian Affairs in 1959," *op. cit.*, p. 50.

[15] *Saskatoon Star-Phoenix*, January 4, 1969.

[16] Within the exclusive jurisdiction of the provinces for unregistered Indians and Metis, and for urban Indians off the reserves. For an examination of the increasing role of provincial services, see *Hawthorn Report*, Vol. 1, p. 199. In practice, a very complex network of legal and financial arrangements has grown up between federal and provincial Governments.

[17] Saskatchewan, *The Indian and Metis Bill: A Speech to Saskatchewan Legislature by the Hon. W. Ross Thatcher*, March 5, 1969, Regina, Queen's Printer, 1969.

[18] *Saskatoon Star-Phoenix*, January 4, 1969.

[19] Thatcher, *op. cit.*, p. 6.

[20] *Ibid., Placement Officer Reports*, and Saskatchewan, Department of Indian and Metis Affairs, 1967-1969.

[21] Department of Citizenship and Immigration, Indian Affairs Branch, *Annual Report*, Saskatchewan Region, 1961, p. 4.

[22] In *Down and Out in Paris and London*, Harmondsworth, Middlesex, Penguin Books Ltd. 1969.

[23] The researcher has met with considerable openness on the part of the custodians, who are most cooperative in supplying the most confidential information, with little apparent concern for the use to be made of the material.

[24] Salvation Army custodians agree with this conclusion.

[25] In fact, the Salvation Army maintains close relations with the Department of Social Welfare.

[26] *Salvation Army Hostel Files* and *Interview*, June 30, 1969. The files have a "nationality" entry. In many cases it is left blank or "French," "Canadian," etc., are filled in. Since most Indians have Europeanized names, it is not likely that an exact number was obtained.

[27] *Interview*, March 30, 1970. Evening highlights are also provided: handicrafts on Monday; Alcoholics Anonymous on Saturday; and a social evening on Wednesday.

[28] The Friendship Inn has also been a smashing success in terms of interdenominational cooperation.

# 6
## The Limitations of Bureaucratic Services

As the organization increases in size, the struggle for great principles becomes impossible. [Michels]

Bureaucratic organizations face hard times when their policy environments change suddenly and irrevocably. They are not built for unexpected occurrences, like the awakening of a group. On the contrary, internal specialization and personnel procedures render them hostile to change. Specialties, however ill-suited to the task at hand, must nonetheless be protected by a guarantee of job security. Cooperation inside a bureaucracy is never easy to achieve, and anyone who would alter, and therefore threaten, "workable" routines must make a good case, and preferably a mild one. The maintenance of the system is the basic point of departure, and the chief good.[1]

The Indian Affairs Branch, in the course of the last decade, has been faced with unprecedented demands at every level. In the urban field, its attempts to adapt to a changed situation are of immediate interest. Four items will be discussed briefly: the level of cooperation between the Indian Affairs Branch and its provincial counterpart, the Indian-Metis Branch; the repercussions of the hiring of native personnel; the question of 'bureaucracy and participation'; and the failure of the IAB to develop new policies in the urban field.

### Local Cooperation
Despite a public show of solidarity, some in-fighting goes on both within and between the IAB and IMB. This manifests itself in several different forms. First, personality problems intensify a natural tendency toward empire-building in petty officialdom.

117

The job placement field is a case in point. Since contacts with important businessmen in the city are involved, status and reputation give an edge to rivalries. Usually the incidents involve one placement officer discrediting the candidate of another placement officer by broadcasting stories of unreliability to the potential employers. Thus the senior Indian Affairs Branch officer in Saskatoon explained that "the young boys" in the Indian-Metis Branch were sabotaging the atmosphere of good will he had laboriously worked to create with local employers in the potash industry by sending over inexperienced and unemployable Indians and Metis.

In reply, the Indian-Metis Branch officials contend that the Indian Affairs Branch has been unwilling to share the prerogative of nominating Indians for positions and has given the IMB a bad reputation. "Empire-building" by agencies is to be expected; it is certainly not the exclusive preserve of the two major Indian-Metis agencies in the city of Saskatoon.

*In general however, there is a high degree of cooperation between the* IAB *and the* IMB. The latter has discreetly placed the emphasis of its program on non-registered Indians and Metis, leaving the IAB unchallenged in the treaty Indian field. The IAB, for its part, is only too happy to have part of the crushing burden of Indian administration lifted from its shoulders. Officially it continually emphasizes the joint responsibility of federal and provincial agencies:

> In the circumstances in which we are confronted today we are literally working in partnership with provincial authorities, Canada Manpower, and other federal agencies in the field of placement and relocation. There must be maintained a liaison with other federal and provincial agencies in the placement field. In Saskatoon, the first referral of potential employees should be to the Canada Manpower (CMC) and/or the provincial Indian-Metis Branch. . . .
>
> Indian Affairs personnel in any way connected with employment placement should put public relations with potential employers and agencies with whom they are cooperating high on their list of priorities.[2]

In general, a good working relationship has developed, cemented by the close friendship of the native people employed in the two agencies.

The IAB and IMB retain a high level of unchallenged discretion in dealing with their constituency. The legitimacy of the total administrative structure of the IAB may be undermined; the Indian revolution may be in full swing; vast changes may be taking place on many reserves. But in the city the IAB and IMB officials are acknowledged as the experts in the field by the other bureaucracies. Sniping is common from the radical left, but agencies have not yet been subjected to serious questioning. Indeed, the relative calm surrounding IAB operations in cities led the *Hawthorn Report* to suggest that it take the lead in facilitating successful urbanization.[3]

## Native Personnel

In the policy environment of Indian Affairs in Canada, it was practically inevitable that a displacement of goals from organizational aims to adherence to internal rules, would occur at an early date. The purposes (controlling the Indians; developing self-support among the Indians) were too general to yield performance criteria; hence the easiest way to gain recognition within the IAB was to follow procedures as closely as possible. The margin of safety lay with the field manual. Red tape, in short, became the indicator of achievement, the more, the better. Mountains of information have been collected and sent to Ottawa, but rarely was it even meant to be processed. Manuals lay out in the greatest detail the specific duties, terms of reference, and reporting procedures for officers who have had nothing to report. Indian Affairs is an extreme case of an organization where rules fulfil symbolic as well as utilitarian functions.[4]

From this perspective, the emphasis on the hiring of Indians and Metis has sent shock waves down the organizational charts. That many native people have acquired high status positions is especially distressing, since they "have not followed the rules" to get there. Both implicitly and explicitly, such a practice is a threat to the positions and careers of white officials, and has exercised a disquieting effect on both the IAB and IMB bureaucracies at the local level.[5]

Many books could be written about the deadening atmosphere of suppressed hostility in the whispering corridors of the IAB. The white officials, particularly the placement officers, are very much upset at the sight of native people obtaining positions of responsibility without the requisite qualifications and experience. To a certain extent they are perfectly justified. Although many native people in the offices are very well-equipped, the great demand for Indian personnel has led to the wholesale employment of individuals whose sole distinction is native ancestry. The agencies have placed young natives in important positions where efficiency is absolutely necessary for sound office management, and it is only too embarrassingly the case that many of these jobs are done badly, slowing down the work of the entire office staff.

The Indian Affairs Branch office did not, however, need to employ Indians and Metis to be branded as inefficient. It has long had a notorious reputation as the slowest, most trivial-minded Agency of the federal Government. The stories of neglect, of letters remaining unanswered, of hostility toward the clientele, of the employment of utterly incompetent veterans, are legendary among Indians and Government officials alike.[6] The crux of the matter is that the employment of Indians and Metis has placed the white administrators on the defensive. It should also not be forgotten that the publication of the Government's *New Policy*, outlining the abolition of the Indian Affairs Branch section within five years, has not helped to allay anxieties among white officials. The deadline is likely to be extended indefinitely, but the relative impact on Indian and white career expectations is striking.[7]

Given the tremendous demand for native skills, the Indians and Metis who are employed in the IAB are eminently mobile; the *New Policy* does not adversely affect their careers in any way. The middle-aged white official, on the other hand, finds the prospect, however remote, of moving to another federal agency most unpleasing (not least because he may have to accustom himself to a job where self-righteousness is absent). In any case the Branch appears increasingly less prestigious at the local level. There is an unmistakable loss of confidence and nerve among the white officials *vis-à-vis* the Indians and Metis who are now working alongside them. When their native colleagues are not present, they will confide their apprehensions and frustrations to the visitor.

On their side, the Indians and Metis are unsure of themselves and complain about the "attitudes" of the white officials. "He knows a lot," confided an Indian counselling officer about a white colleague, "but it's the attitude that's wrong. Since his father was an Agent, he can tell stories of the earlier days, and has records to back them up. But he resents the Indians and

120

treats them like children." Whites and Indians in the office laugh and joke together while intensely hating each other; below the chit-chat, the tensions of the post-colonial situation are acute. On one occasion, after I had arrived early in the morning for an interview with an IAB official, my apparent sympathy for the IAB and the predicament of its white careerists completely upset the work pattern of the entire office. First, all the white officials drifted in to complain; the Indians followed with tales of resentment, unrest, and discourtesies.

It is important to understand that the tensions do not arise out of substantive issues or decisions regarding the treatment of the native population as a whole. Both the white and the native officials in these offices agree on the nature of services that are offered. The services are to be as bureaucratically oriented as possible. Despite the jealousies and the problem of human relations in the offices, both groups share a common life style. Both see themselves as superior to the general native population. Both are certain that they are meant to civilize the masses, giving the native people themselves as little actual control in decision-making as possible. The net effect of the white-native bickering is to depress the office atmosphere, lower efficiency even further, and undermine what little morale may have existed.

### Bureaucracy and Participation

Federal Government documents clearly endorse the principles of "participation," "self-help," "partnership," and "consultation" in *all* programs dealing with the indigenous population:

> I stress and underline the need for full consultation with the Indians. . . . They, through their own leaders, must be partners with us in charting a new approach and new programs. . . . The essential ingredient for the full success of all our operations [is] the full participation by the Indian people under their own leaders. . . . [8]

The provincial Government has been no less anxious to point out its commitment to "self-help" programs. [9]

In practice, however, any self-help project that demands independent decision-making powers for the natives is awarded the most hostile reception. The clearest example of this in Saskatoon was the official agencies' attitude toward the Indian and Metis Development Society (Big Bear Gallery), founded in January

1969. The society grew out of continuous conversations between white and Indian city residents. It had no model; little rhetoric was involved; as ideas jelled, an institution took form. Within six months it had opened a large building in an attractive part of town; it had become the leading source of controversy among native organizers in the city, and had generated widespread support in the community at large. It was the only organization in the city which seriously threatened to become an independently-financed urban organization controlled and directed by local Indians and Metis. Whites were involved, but the Constitution limited their participation to 30 per cent of the voting shares, and similar voting weight on the Board of Directors. Here finally was one organization where the bureaucracies were not in control. The Indians opened a little handicraft store to generate savings for the Society; it obtained notice from the University that it would honour employment recommendations. Its building was designed as a museum, and was large enough to act as a social centre. The IAB and IMB were not consulted at any stage in the development of the Society.

Catastrophic errors in judgment and personnel selection eventually undermined the project, but during the summer these were hidden from the public. It appeared to the outside that a powerful movement had begun and that a power base in the community was being established. The reaction of the IAB was clear and effective. The vilification of persons on the Board of Directors was a first tactic, and one not to be underestimated, given the control of the IAB over the daily lives of many natives in the city. Another was the withholding of information vital to an organization in the opening stages, when many people have to be contacted quickly. Only the IAB and the IMB had the records and statistics needed to compile address lists and background information on specific reserves and organizations. Although their files are shared with many other institutions, they remained closed to the Big Bear Gallery. Thirdly, the IAB withheld loans and funds at a crucial stage of development, advising that self-help projects must prove themselves before they could be assisted. When asked what "proving themselves" meant, the Indians were told, "self-sufficiency." The IAB gave no reply to the rejoinder that a development loan would hardly be necessary when self-sufficiency had been attained.[10]

Panic set in at the IAB when the Big Bear Gallery drew up plans for a residence for high school students who came into the

122

city. The staff was to be provided by members of the Board of Directors, or someone selected by them and approved by the students. Now one of the most important functions of the IAB office in Saskatoon is the counselling of Indian high school children who come in from the reserve to attend local schools, and who board at homes approved by the IAB counsellors. When it appeared at last that a suitable person had been found to set up the residence, the IAB was most upset. Days and even nights were spent trying to dissuade the woman chosen from cooperating with the Society, and telling her that she was sure to be cheated if she trusted it. On the other hand, financial help was offered for the project *if the* IAB *controlled it.* As the official said, he had only the interests of the employee and the children at heart. "Why," the woman asked, "do you feel threatened?" To this there was no reply. Similarly, although a direct appeal to the Minister of Municipal Affairs yielded a small grant to cover expenses for a few months, the local IMB (with the exception of one officer) spared no effort to discredit the Society and its members.

Clearly, if the bureaucracies take the word "participation" at all seriously, they have something in mind other than assisting social action projects. Using a breakdown employed in another case to analyze the American War on Poverty, and the Maximum Feasible Participation clause in particular, four forms of "participation" can be distinguished: policy-making, program development, employment, and social action.[11] The IAB and the IMB obviously lay chief stress on "employment," the other forms being derivative from the employment of native people in the official bureaucracies. Once in the IAB, Indian and Metis bureaucrats are expected to construe the term "social action" in the narrowest possible way. In practice, this means the rejection of any programs not sponsored by the bureaucracy itself. "Red power" in any form is anathema; in the view of the Branch, it includes all activities ranging from conflict tactics as proposed by Saul Alinsky, to extremely moderate organizations such as the Indian and Metis Development Society. Any concept or project that views poverty as a function of powerlessness will be rejected by the IAB. Self-help and cooperative efforts in the community under ethnic control are taken to be inherently "political." The bureaucracies then do not distinguish among the social action programs that they condemn. A "third-force" status of groups who equally reject militance and present bureaucratic approaches, who attempt social action projects with the support of less militant Indians and Metis, will be condemned out of hand.[12]

That leaves a narrow room for "permissible" community action. The IAB and the IMB limit their support to functional or non-profit community organizations, benign neighbourhood improvement associations such as sewing clubs, and Indian and Metis organizations that serve as social brokerage groups for the Government. None of these are meant to have an independent power base; they are to serve as adjuncts to bureaucratic and service-oriented programs. This philosophy is shown most clearly in the Friendship Centre concept. Both the federal and provincial Governments have been impressed with the functioning of Friendship Centres in urban centres. According to the Minister of Municipal Affairs in Saskatchewan, "they show results."[13] They are considered an integral part of a successful urban program by IAB officials in Saskatoon, who lamented the failure in 1968 of the first attempt to establish one, and applaud the efforts recently underway to develop another in the city.

The model for Friendship Centres in other locales was provided by Winnipeg, which by 1960 had a well-functioning referral centre for native transients.[14] Prince Albert, Saskatchewan, followed with the establishment of the Indian and Metis Service Council of Prince Albert, which embodied the main principles of its Winnipeg counterpart. Reverend Adam Cuthand listed many functions for the Prince Albert Council – job placement, leadership training, housing relocations – but the emphasis was on counselling and the referral of Indians and Metis to the available federal and provincial services.[15] As the Centres spread, the Constitutions continued to allow the Directors much scope for action. Thus one close observer found them involved in many different kinds of community services:

> The Friendship Centre is the only agency primarily oriented ...and aimed at providing the Indian with a place where he is accepted socially and where he can find advice and direction, with understanding. In visiting the Centres, I found them involved (in counselling, court work, employment, housing, referrals, recreation, clothing centre, Indian Clubs) and overloaded.[16]

The advice was to redirect them to the original purpose, referral, rather than have them take up activities provided by the bureaucracies. The Centre should act as a liaison unit. Thus, although the "Centres should aim at being entirely run by Indians with non-Indians acting only in an advisory capacity," they should serve as informal extensions of bureaucratic channels. An informal atmosphere should draw the disoriented transients into a native establishment which is much more likely to communicate with them. Once "off the streets," the native person can be found by the relevant government office:

> The Centre should make full use of the Planning Council and social agencies, such as the Family Bureau, Children's Aid, and Neighbourhood Services, and these agencies should have an Indian person on their staff to provide liaison.[17]

In no way, however, are the Centres to be political. The provincial Government of Saskatchewan will have nothing to do with native community institutions that even suggest "Red Power." Indeed, the fear that Dr. Howard Adams, the Metis leader of some notoriety, was associated with Big Bear Gallery, had to be laboriously allayed before any grant would be forthcoming. If a Friendship Centre takes up the idea of independent social action, its financial support will be removed.[18]

Many factors combine to produce the intransigence of the IAB toward new ideas in community development. First, it responds to both a public and governmental fear that any form of ethnic separatism in cities is inherently revolutionary. Mention has already been made of its housing program, which is explicitly assimilatory. Community development on the reserves is seen as a conditioning experience for the adaptation to the existing organizational structure in the city. In the urban environment, it will not tolerate a separate constituency.

**The Failure of Policy Development**

There would be room for experimentation even within these limitations, if the Indian Affairs agencies possessed imagination and the will to innovate. The factor of immobility is therefore as deserving of explanation as is the overall conservatism. Part of the answer lies in the peculiarity of a large bureaucratic organization charged with a paternalistic caretaker function. The Indian Affairs Branch administered to an ethnic group that was totally submerged until its recent revival in the 1960's. In the absence of pressure from below, reality could be comfortably ignored. For almost a century, there was no feedback process, no error-information-correction system, and consequently no adjustment of programs in view of errors. Moreover, the nature of the constituency meant that there was no serious challenge to powerful secular interests in Canada; the IAB thus failed to attract administrators of a high level of competence or dedication.[19] At the same time, a wide range of influential political groups – farmers, Churches, taxpayers in general – had an economic attachment to the status quo in Indian Affairs. The result has been the creation of a truly amazing monument to inefficiency and personal tyranny. The social and bureaucratic milieu and the IAB stood in direct contradiction to the policy environment which produced innovation in other governmental agencies. The brand of paternalism and total administration practised by the IAB and sanctioned by society precluded an enlightened response to the unexpected demands of a long-docile clientele.

By 1960, however, the IAB was called upon to be *the* initiating unit in Indian affairs and to lead public opinion in the Indian's search for equality in Canadian society. Officially, the Branch was up-graded in the Department of Indian Affairs and Northern Development, and its philosophy changed from paternalism to partnership. Sincere attempts were made to recruit personnel who knew something about community development. Above all, a successful effort has been made to employ native people and to have them participate in drawing up and implementing programs.

Why then has the effort failed to generate a creative response to urbanization? First, much deadwood of the old school survived in the IAB, despite the change in rhetoric. The hard-core paternalist will never change. Self-help on the reserves is traumatic enough; adventure in the city is inconceivable.

Second, there is a very real lack of expertise. The field is entirely unexplored, and the placement officers simply do not have the time to carry out systematic research. Moreover, the IAB is low on talent, for its imminent demise has frightened away the better minds. Similarly, the repellent reputation of the IAB and IMB scarcely makes for comfortable relations with the academics likely to interest themselves in the field. On the provincial side, Saskatchewan has a special problem: the late Premier Ross Thatcher decimated the ranks of the civil service and left everyone too terrified to act. The Indians and Metis who are hired are much too involved in *Affluent* affairs to have the time for the study required in the formation of new concepts.

Third, the essential prerequisite for a responsive bureaucracy, that is, a critical and active constituency, still does not exist. On many reserves, progress toward self-government has been made, but this has not occurred in the cities. The native minority in Saskatoon has no resource-base to create the independence required to challenge the bureaucracy. Unfortunately for the larger segment of the native population, the *Affluent* have little complaint with the present bureaucratic *ennui*. Thus their employment has little effect in facilitating a greater flexibility in approach. The *Affluent* have successfully made the transition to the city and project their own experience as a model for their native brothers. Since available services have accommodated their needs so remarkably well, why should they not do the same for the rest? Moreover, their lucrative positions depend on the continuation of the bureaucratic approach. Self-help and social action outside their class threaten their status as much as that of the white administrators. The *Affluent* are sufficiently lucid not to kill the goose. . . .

## Conclusion: Missionaries from the Outside World

In general, there is probably more cooperation among all the agencies in this field than one might have expected. Rivalries there are, but by and large all groups share a common attitude toward the Indian and Metis population. All of them, from the Indian Affairs Branch down to the Salvation Army, are missionaries from the outside world. All consider the Indians and Metis as deviants to be brought back to some kind of secular or religious fold. The "caretakers" of the native population of Canada desperately want the clients to adopt the behaviour and values of the larger white society.[20]

Herbert Gans makes a distinction among three forms of caretakers: first, the service-oriented caretaker, who helps the client achieve goals that he could not achieve by himself; second, the market-oriented caretaker, who sells the client what he wants; and third, the missionary caretaker.[21] In the case of the Indians and Metis, the first two are simply not to be found. The whole society, in its relations with the Indian and Metis minority via the caretakers, is infused with a desire to bring the deviant group into an acceptance of its norms. Whatever the effect on the Indians and Metis, it does provide a very considerable source of cooperation and goodwill among the agencies operating in the urban field – subject to the limitations imposed by personal and

127

confessional rivalries within the broader goal of converting the native. As we have seen, the employment of the *Affluent* Indians in the official bureaucracies has not decisively changed this attitude toward the Indian and Metis population as a whole. To a very large extent, the *Affluent* share the goals of the white agencies and churches. They also look at the minority from above. "Trait-making" has all the ring of a joint crusade. The Plough and the Bible still go hand in hand.

---

[1] Victor A. Thompson, *Modern Organization*, New York, Knopf, 1961, p. 19.

[2] Department of Citizenship and Immigration, Indian Affairs Branch, *Employment and Relocation Programs, Saskatchewan Region*, 1967, p. 2.

[3] *Hawthorn Report*, Vol. 1, pp. 12-13. Cf. Dunning, "Some Aspects of Indian Administration," *op. cit.*, pp. 216-233.

[4] Robert K. Merton, "Bureaucratic Structure and Personality," *Reader in Bureaucracy*, ed. R. Merton *et. al*, Glencoe, Ill., Free Press, 1951, pp. 166-168.

[5] Chester Barnard, "The Functions of Status Systems," *Bureaucracy*, p. 243.

[6] See Dunning, "Some Aspects of Indian Administration," *op. cit.*, p. 222, where she compares the IAB to the British Government's Indian Civil Service. Unlike the latter, the low status of Indian administration resulted in a less selective administrative corps with a consequent lower interest in achievement.

[7] The Ministry of State has greatly expanded its activities in the field of Indian Affairs since the White Paper [Author's note].

[8] Indian Affairs Branch, *Senior Field Officer's Conference*, Ottawa, January, 1964, p. 20. Also Indian Affairs Branch, Administration of Indian Affairs, *op. cit.*, pp. 10, 17, 20; and *National Superintendent's Conference*, September, 1961, p. 6. These are only isolated examples of the tremendous emphasis put on these slogans.

[9] Thatcher, *op. cit.*. p. 8.

[10] Later a project more to the IAB's liking, the Friendship Centre, obtained a large grant, even though it had neither directors nor members.

[11] Ralph M. Kramer, *The Participation of the Poor*, Englewood Cliffs, Prentice-Hall, 1969, p. 14ff.

[12] For similar problems in the United States, see Richard A. Cloward, "The War on Poverty: Are the Poor Left Out?" *The Nation*, Vol. 201, No. 3, August 2, 1965. Also see G. E. Mortimore, "The Indians Are Losing Another War," *Toronto Globe and Mail*, December 22, 1966: "Should the Government hire professional troublemakers to launch a revolution against poverty . . . or should aid to the poor be doled out quietly through conventional civil service and welfare agency channels?" This article goes on to show the dilemma faced by the IAB when it confronted the problem of community development.

[13] The federal Government and some provincial Governments, spurred by public demand, hired a corps of men called community development officers, whose job was to aid the Indians in giving shape to their wants and grievances, to stir them from apathy – in fact to make them discontented – and help them mobilize for action. Some of the community development officers did so well – stimulating the Indians to clamour for better schools, jobs, housing, and health services – that they alarmed the line administrative officers of the Indian Affairs Branch, whose aims were much different from their own. *Interview*, May 20, 1969.

[14] *The Indian News*, Vol. 10, No. 4, 1967, for an examination of several Centres across Canada.

[15] *The Western Producer*, April 28, 1960.

[16] Mr. Walter Currie, Chairman of the Indian-Eskimo Associations' Committee on Indians and the City, *National Conference on Indians and the City*, Winnipeg, October 7-9, 1966, p. 13.

[17] *The Indian and Eskimo Association of Canada Bulletin*, Vol. 7, No. 5.

[18] One of the contributing factors in the decline of Big Bear Gallery was its association with Howard Adam's radical Metis Society, in an attempt to share part of the rent burden. The association generated enormous suspicion and ruled out further Government assistance, at least until the Gallery could prove that the link was definitely broken.

[19] *Hawthorn Report*, Vol. 1, pp. 360-386. See also Dunning, "Aspects of Indian Policy," *op. cit.*, who makes the same point.

[20] "Caretakers," generally speaking, can be defined as institutions and individuals who offer various kinds of care to, in this case, the native population. They include people and agencies who offer medical and/or psychiatric treatment; occupational, social, and psychological counselling; economic assistance; social aid or information, or advice in general; as well as educational and quasi-educational programs intended to benefit their users.

[21] Gans, *op. cit.*, pp. 142-145.

# 7
## Perpetuation of
## the Poverty Cycle

It is not through lack of services that the government agencies have failed to accomplish their objectives. However, misjudgment of the ways in which Indians can and ought to be brought into city life has meant that administrators can only point to isolated successes, while the overall situation progressively deteriorates. The transformation of the kinship structure; the racial exclusiveness of the native minority; and the dependence of the native people on white society: all operate in the urban environment within the specific orientation of the poverty programs. The role of these programs in creating and perpetuating the structure of Indian poverty in an urban context must now be examined.

### The Old Boy Network of the Affluent
The most striking feature of the poverty programs is the special treatment afforded migrants from the "leading families" on the reserve. The same generalization holds for the Metis from the more prosperous families. On the one hand, they are the chief beneficiaries of services for off-reserve Indians, while on the other, their rewards are distributed and "arranged" through connections with the more powerful native leaders and their white colleagues. The force of this "old boy network" is shown by job placement and housing statistics. Among 1240 placements by the Saskatoon Indian Affairs Branch in the years 1967-1969, members of the "leading families" either do not appear, or immediately gain access to good positions. A relatively low educational level does not appear to be a crucial impediment to satisfactory employment connections of these applicants. Many of the children of these families do have Grade xi or above,

since in their background emphasis has been placed on education. Whether they are objectively qualified or not, however, they are recommended to someone in one or another agency. If a position becomes available, it is soon found by an *Affluent* Indian, often one whose only qualification is his connections. It can be stated as a rule that every *Affluent* Indian head of household will be approached by either a government agency or an Indian organization for a job, and that his sons and daughters, who usually have Grade x or above, will find suitable employment. The girls will be hired as secretaries or typists in government offices; the sons will obtain positions in the bureaucracies or Indian-Metis organizations as did their fathers.

A remarkable development in the last few years is the increased effectiveness of the *Affluent* "old boy network" in obtaining status positions. Before 1967 – that is, before the urban *Affluent* had consolidated into a tight urban status formation – there were file references to IAB and IMB referral and counselling services for "leading family" heads of households.[1] After this date these entries become much less frequent as the informal process of cooptation and inter-*Affluent* recommendation has become more effective. The official IAB and IMB Placement Programs, therefore, are services for the "other" Indians. Children of the *Affluent* often come to the agencies for jobs and may be officially "placed," but the job selection is carefully regulated in their interests. Since their parents are "dependable" (and powerful), it is assumed that the offspring will also be reliable.

As the number of native people with high school education increases, "connections" are becoming increasingly valuable to ensure employment. Low as enrolment at the high school level remains, the "leading families" form a very small percentage of the total Indian population, and must protect their positions. In the immediate future, they need not worry; but a burst of white indifference could severely affect the demand for native personnel. Fortunately for this group, the challenge from below is nonexistent. The marginal position of the overall Indian-Metis job applicant permits an easy functioning of the old school tie.

The list of off-reserve housing grants yields similar findings. It reads like an Indian *Who's Who* for Saskatchewan, and stops after fifty-eight names.[2] Of the sixteen approved for Saskatoon, twelve heads of households were involved in poverty programs and Indian-Metis organizations. As in employment, the *Affluent* are not confronted by a major housing problem upon arrival in

131

the city. Indeed, the Indians who moved into Saskatoon with the expansion of the IAB office had obtained off-reserve housing prior to relocation, so that they immediately obtained fine houses in the newer neighbourhoods. It is worth recalling that these grants are valued at $10,000 per family, whereas relocation grants are estimated to cost $459.73 per family, and employment placement a mere $13.88 per person. The budgetary priorities are obvious.

Given the pan-Indian social network in the city and the certainty of obtaining good employment and housing, the chief need of the *Affluent* is psychological satisfaction in the urban environment. These identity problems, however, can also be resolved. The *Affluent* Indians and Metis in the city can scarcely avoid becoming "leaders" of government sponsored and financed organizations. The Friendship Centre, the Federation of Saskatchewan Indians, the Big Bear Gallery, the Metis Society, the Indian Urban Association, the Saskatoon Indian Committee, etc. – all offer the opportunity to create myths about the past, to complain about the present, and to go home feeling at one with the Indians and the world. The identity crisis itself is given societal recognition.

The loose informal association that characterized the "leading families" and the *Affluent* Indians in the urban environment is therefore deeply integrated into the structure of the poverty programs. If, as sometimes happens, an *Affluent* family has difficulties, massive assistance from the Department of Social Welfare or from the Indian Affairs Branch will be made available. Such interventions are arranged in the corridors of the agencies, on terms of equality between Indian and white colleagues. There is no grovelling for assistance and no expectation of downward mobility into the *Welfare* grouping. The thrust of the Indian poverty programs is to grant extraordinary assistance to the *Affluent* families and individuals via relocation grants, off-reserve housing, furniture grants and assured access to government-sponsored native organizations. Entrenched in the bureaucracies, the *Affluent* find their economic, social and psychological needs satisfied by and integrated into available programs.

## Welfare Indians and the Dole

With several important exceptions, the Indians and Metis outside the 'leading families' are given predictable treatment when they come to the official and voluntary agencies. The poverty programs themselves have been outlined in the previous chapter; it is now necessary to take a closer look at their clientele. Since employment is the heart of trait-making at this level, the analysis now relies heavily on the IAB Placement Officer Reports. Out of a total of 1,275 entries, it was possible to examine 1,240 cases in depth. Information was not complete in the other cases.

First, it cannot be overemphasized that the vast majority of job placements were "temporary." Of the 915 men and 216 women placed, only 43 and 12 respectively found "permanent" positions. Though some people holding temporary jobs were able to retain them, the employment prospects for Indians can be seen to be very bleak indeed: the employment structure for native people is unpromising.

It is most unusual for women to obtain jobs other than as waitresses or domestics, and both categories of work are extremely poorly paid. Of 215 women, 169 were placed in these positions. However, if female applicants had achieved a Grade XII education; if they were young (between the ages of 20 and 30) and unmarried, they stood a good chance of employment in a government agency, or as secretaries in the private sector. The number of Indian women with these qualifications is small, 28 for the two years 1967-69, but it is by far the best situated group in the Placement Files. Placement Officers agree that the only consistently marketable group of job applicants are the Grade XII women.

Male applicants were consistently worse off. Although they had a higher educational level than the reserve Indians in their agencies, the average was not more than Grade VIII, and twice as many women proportionally had reached Grade XII.[3] Half as many government jobs went to men as to women, and of those that did go to men, two-thirds were temporary jobs in parks and recreation areas. In general, male applicants were employed in railway gangs, on construction sites, and in industrial and service industries of every kind.

The statistics yield much new information and some trends, but they must be used with the greatest caution. They add insight only when they are integrated into follow-up information on the people placed. It is not enough to know that people obtained jobs. One must also find out if they kept them. Unfortunately, it was not possible to go beyond a sample of the total. Of 23 permanent placements, only three remained after a period of three months. Eighteen per cent of temporary employees placed between April 1 and August 30, 1969, stayed at their jobs.[4] The one group that maintained stable permanent positions was composed of the Grade XII female migrants who worked as clerks or typists in a governmental or business office. Men with Grade XII, although usually placed in positions comparable to the females, did not show the same tenacity.

Interviews with IAB Placement Officers revealed a working assumption on their part that the vast majority of Indians employed will not remain on the job. They therefore save the most promising openings for individuals who appear to be reliable, and give little attention to the ordinary applicant. In some cases, reliability is determined by educational achievement; this is particularly true in the case of young single girls with a high school education. In the vast majority of cases, however, educational level is far less important than the Placement Officer's character estimate of the individual. The potash industry provides a case in point. The Chief Placement Officer of the IAB in Saskatoon indicated quite clearly that he would not recommend anyone to the potash industry who does not appear to be dependable.

*The decisive fact is the marginality of the Indian labour force.* Employers know that; the Placement Officers know that; and the Indians know that. By law, private industry on government contracts is compelled to hire 5 per cent of Indians and Metis,[5] but many firms had already made a point of showing their public spirit by hiring a certain number each year, before the passage of this legislation. They are not, however, forced to keep them if they miss work or in other ways prove to be unreliable. There are many white workers ready to fill the positions of the native employees. Despite a tacit understanding between the Placement Officers and the employers that the majority of placements will not work out, the employers cooperate with the Government in the belief that exposure to a work situation will pay long-term dividends in the building of character.

## Patterns of Migration Among the Welfare Indians and Metis

The combination of official encouragement to work and economic marginality has resulted in differing patterns of migration into the *Welfare* stratum. One that is easily documented in the Placement Files involves groups of people who come in from the reserves, get a short-term job, and are never seen again in the Placement office. Although employment lasted only a few weeks, these individuals return to the city, becoming chronic visitors at the Salvation Army and Indian houses. Thus in September 1967, two brothers, one married and one single, came in from a reserve and were placed in positions which they quickly lost. In the summer of 1969, both got on the Salvation Army list and their names no longer appeared in the job placement records. Another younger brother then joined them in the city, spending three days every month at the Salvation Army, but not venturing into the employment office. In another case, several "indigent" members of a reserve turned up in January 1968 to look for jobs for the first time. The Salvation Army records show that they had been regular visitors there since 1964 and 1965. Job placement was a brief and isolated episode in their urban existence – once it was over, the Salvation Army pattern again recurred.

If anything can be suggested about this first pattern, it is that most Indians appear to become chronic visitors at the Salvation Army and Indian houses after a job placement has introduced them to the city. Work in the city gives them a toe-hold in the urban environment. Once they are established, they enter on the fringes of city life, not interested in work, but able to eke out a subsistence in the labyrinth of voluntary agencies such as the Salvation Army, the Friendship Inn and friends whom they meet in town. Most of these natives have merely made Saskatoon their centre of operations – they do not reside in the city all the time, but travel around the countryside or return to the reserve when the going in Saskatoon gets rough. Nonetheless, they must be considered part of the urban community because they put pressure on the resources of the city; because they use urban institutions; and because they are deeply woven into the ethnic stratification system.

This group should be distinguished from genuine transients such as students or hospital patients. Their migration pattern is also very different from that of the native people who never approach the Indian Affairs Branch office at all to try to get jobs. The Salvation Army records reveal a large number of this latter type of migrant, particularly from the far northern agencies where educational and skill levels are even lower than in the more southern agencies; or from reserves such as Key and Cote where social and personal disorganization has been particularly severe.[6] Most members of this latter group appear to stay at most for several weeks in the city, as they drift continuously among the various urban centres, reserves and northern communi-

135

ties.[7] This group also uses city resources and may have some difficulties with the law. But its association with the urban environment is so slight and its involvement in the social structure so minimal, that it must be classified as "transient."

A second pattern of *Welfare* migration associated with the Indian Affairs Branch Placement Office involves a group that leads a more stable existence, based on relatives in the city and more frequent visits to the office. This is particularly true of migrants from the nearby agencies (Duck Lake, Battleford, Sturgeon Lake) which have high rates of migration to the city. Thus in May 1968, eight men came in from a neighbouring reserve; two stayed at the Salvation Army and the other six stayed with relatives who were struggling to make a go of it in the city. They remained in the city and became well established in the communal residence. They sought employment three times, although in each job they lasted only a few weeks. No attempt was made to escape *Welfare* status. These bouts of employment, life with the relatives, and the occasional application for clothing and living allowances, were viewed as an entering wedge into more stable types of welfare: unemployment insurance and perhaps co-habitation with a girl drawing checks from the Department of Social Welfare.

People with this orientation take advantage of upgrading and, where possible, vocational training. The expansion in these programs has been spectacular. Canada Manpower, the Indian Affairs Branch, and the Indian-Metis Branch have all emphasized that training, education and employment form a unified strategy. But it is illusory to conclude that a more educated work force will necessarily increase social mobility.

There is certainly a tremendous need for education, and it is encouraging that the parents, at least, are going to school, and that allowances are paid to native participants of all ages in order to stimulate the appetite for learning. However, it would be utopian to place much emphasis on the short-run importance of these upgrading programs. There is no evidence as yet that they result in a more highly-motivated work force. In the long run, there could be important effects on the children, but at the moment it appears safe to conclude that the adult educational programs fulfill an immediate financial need for the *Welfare* natives. Among the 1,240 IAB placements in the years 1967-1969, 30 individuals had vocational training. A follow-up on these cases did not reveal consistently longer job tenure. The two girls who were represented worked as maids; the visits to the Salvation Army by the men were roughly similar in frequency to those of the non-trained.[8]

Employment placement programs, together with educational and training services, are necessary but not sufficient inputs for social mobility among the *Welfare* Indians and Metis. The present study has not found significant evidence that this peripheral contact with the institutions of the larger society suddenly instills a determination to work, save and create a stable family environment in the city. Implicitly, poverty programs recognize the difficulty of change at this level by concentrating their resources on specific families above the welfare line. Some hope is rested in "sociological" institutions such as the Friendship Centre and the Friendship Inn which take the *Welfare* native people off the streets. The conclusion, therefore, concerning the effects of the poverty programs on the *Welfare*, is that they do not foster upward mobility; in the immediate future little impact on the native social structure can be anticipated.

### Placement Officers and the Anomic

IAB and IMB Placement Officers have a stoical attitude toward their clientele. Epictetus himself would be proud of the sighs accompanying their endless authorizations of grocery and lodging allowances. They are above getting unduly upset at the poor follow-up statistics. However, they do single out a few individuals and families for lavish attention. These may not necessarily be better equipped for relocation than the average native migrant; they may even have poor job records or be much disliked in another agency. The Placement Officer, for whatever reason, is impressed with their stated desire to relocate, and feels that they are "promising."

The decision to "adopt" such an individual or family is intensely personal: it is based entirely on the discretion of the Placement Officer. The usual rationale given is the evidence of tenacity, demonstrated by their surviving for some months in the urban environment without special assistance. However, there is no way to decide objectively on the basis of so broad a principle. The Placement Officer may simply like the native person in question. In the case of Harvey Lang, this appears to have been the decisive factor in catapulting him to a status position in the city, and ultimately into the ranks of the Indian leadership.

The Lang case was unusually conducive to social mobility

137

because of his educational and family background. Nonetheless, the Senior Placement Officer at the IAB would not risk recommending him for a status position; an IMB counterpart took the chance and succeeded. The situation in more typical cases among the *Anomic* is far more complex. Here even the possibility of status employment is out of the question. The individual or family will be marginal in the labour force and will be confronted by serious social and psychological problems in adapting to city life.

When he "adopts" a family, the Placement Officer incurs a heavy responsibility, both to the Indians and to his own career. Consequently, these relationships are rare – probably less than twenty have been formed *so far* in Saskatoon.[9] They therefore cover only one segment of the *Anomic* – those Indians and Metis who do not gain the favour of the Placement Officer, or who reject this kind of relationship, must get along with the placement and counselling services geared to the *Welfare* grouping. If the *Affluent* in their association with the poverty programs form a select status group, a small number of the *Anomic* are given similarly privileged treatment to induce social mobility. The Placement Officer and his nominee enter into an almost symbiotic relationship during which the official wages war on "Indian" traits. Essentially he attempts to construct a web of associations between himself and the isolated Indian family which will compensate for the break with the reserve family, accustom it to urban technology and prepare it for assimilation into white society. In a different milieu and with different tools, the Placement Officer attempts to create anew the IAB-Indian socialization style that was successful in generating the "leading families" on the reserve.

The importance of this subject must be emphasized. Although they deal with hundreds of native people, the Placement Officers spend the bulk of their time with their "chosen" families. "Trait-making" among the *Welfare* is, in their opinion, a problem whose solution will require many generations, but their "adopted" *Anomic* families must adapt quickly. The most forceful method of presenting the strengths and weaknesses of this approach is through family studies.

### John's Life and Loves

John Beaver and his family came into Saskatoon on Hallowe'en (October 31), 1967, from a northern reserve, determined to seek

138

a new life in the city. Characteristically, they had nothing with them but a few personal effects, and had no money at all. Because five of their seven children were left in a residential school, they gained a somewhat greater freedom of action in Saskatoon. The husband possessed neither skill nor trade, and he had not achieved a Grade VIII education. The wife was responsible for getting the family off the reserve. She was determined that her husband find a job in the city; by 1967, they had heard about programs to assist the Indians to find jobs and housing in the urban environment. On March 4, 1968, the Placement Officer noted in his file:

> Subject came into the city on October 31, 1967 and has been there ever since – has not worked steady and during periods of layoff was a welfare recipient; however, he is determined to make a go of it in the city and his wife is even more determined. They definitely do not wish to return to the reserve; at present they are in need of a fridge, washer, bed, 4 chrome chairs – also need some kitchen utensils and blankets. Subject has been working for Walker Sheet Metal and Roofing, for past two weeks – employer is very satisfied and says subject will have a job with him as long as there are contracts. Makes $2.30 an hour. Have been watching his family closely. Although subject does not have a skill or trade and is not long on education he and his wife have a strong desire to relocate – eventually they wish to find a larger place and move in their family; further, they hope to save enough money to apply for off-reserve housing at a later date.[10]

The Placement Officer was a representative example of the present IAB administrator: loyal to the service; genuinely concerned about "bettering" the Indians; hard-working; and operating in a complex organization with limited resources. He had been with the Saskatoon office for four years and knew more about the city than any other IAB or IMB official. As a white man, he has had some difficulty in adjusting to the increased number of native personnel in the enlarged office; but he remains a dedicated civil servant, with an unforgettable interlude in London with Immigration, and is not unwilling to add his shoulder to the White Man's Burden.

The Placement Officer was very much impressed with the family, and decided to include it in the "twenty families project" of the Indian Affairs Branch. Thereby the family obtained an IAB commitment for preferential treatment, not only in terms of a relocation grant, but also in personal relations with the Placement Officer, who now became a counsellor, advisor and confidant. The family was given an open invitation to call him anytime, day or night, as need arose. The crises were not long in coming. On May 29, 1968, the following entry was made in the report:

> Subject apparently quit his job with Walker Sheet Metal – when asked why he said it was a family affair – apparently had a tiff with his wife over finances and he did this to prove to her that it might be better to return to the reserve. She is still insisting on remaining and he is now looking for another job. Probably this situation could have been averted if we had been fortunate enough to talk to them at the particular time that the disagreement occurred or if they had sought our counselling. Reasoning of subject is difficult to fathom in this situation. Advised to keep in touch regarding employment (Walker's will not rehire) – also lost a house they had located for June 1/68 by not assuring landlord they would be taking. Observation – family affairs play a very important part in the success or failure of a relocation even when all other aspects such as job, etc., are favourable.

The crisis clarified the terms of the relationship between the Placement Officer and the family – *noblesse oblige* on the one side, and gratitude for services rendered on the other. The debacle with Walker Sheet Metal elicited the understanding that assistance would be given, and the valuable contact with the IAB retained, *so long as the Indian family performed favourably according to the guidelines of the white administrator.* The duty of the Indians was to find steady employment, keep away from alcohol, and learn to budget. They were not to become "spoilers," a term the Placement Officer used to refer to "uppity" Indians who had steady jobs (sometimes with the Branch), but who continually sniped at, and tried to undermine the reputation of, the white IAB officials. Secondly, it was made clear that the Indian family was not to engage in any sort of social action. They were the recipients of bureaucratic services; political quiescence was an essential prerequisite for their retention.

As the relationship deepened, the Placement Officer became

increasingly involved with the family. At the same time, he developed a vested interest in the success of this particular relation. His measurement of success was the retention of a good job and the location of better housing. He was therefore particularly annoyed that a relatively good job for a man of that training ($2.30 per hour being considered a fairly good income), had been thrown away over a family squabble.

The domestic incident, however, involved far more than the conventional haggle between man and woman over money. The reserve for the husband was a secure place where problems of industrial and financial discipline did not develop because it lay outside the money economy. The quarrel concerned the relative merits of modernizing values as a whole, and thus indicated the extent to which the family was psychologically split and adrift in the city.

Since Mrs. Beaver refused to move back to the reserve, her husband decided to stay, and the Placement Officer found another job for him with a pipeline company. Another search was made for a house, and the family was registered for low-rental housing. The Placement Officer felt that he had overcome the crisis. On July 26, to help matters along, he authorized the purchase of a rangette and indicated to the family that more furniture would be in the offing if they obtained low-rental housing. By September, however, a note in the Placement Officer's file pointed out growing difficulties:

Five children in residential school in PA – two children under school age with the family – Dahl Agencies has advised this family in line for low-rental housing by end of Oct. – if this comes true they will bring the children into the city to go to school here – John has not been working steady due to inclement weather – his earned pay was only $100.00 for month of August – family received $10.00 from us and $11.00 from welfare – in very desperate straits for next two weeks – John went out of town with Western Pipeline – family trying hard to adjust but John's qualifications make it difficult to get steady employment. Advised Adler (of Manpower) as this is a project family.

A week later, the Placement Officer paid a month's rent of $75, but worse was in store for both parties. Continuing economic troubles probably had something to do with the worsening of the

141

family situation. Toward the end of September, marital problems again arose:

> Phoned myself at 3:15 a.m. on Sunday morning to settle a squabble – Mrs. Beaver took in boarders (against our advice) to try to supplement income – the usual problems arose from too many people in a suite – landlord asked them to leave but they said they would get rid of boarders and he agreed to let them stay – called Beaver myself again last weekend – wife Donna took off on Saturday night and to date have been unable to locate her – husband unable to work because he has to stay with children – seems very broken up about this – John says they will return to reserve on Saturday if she is not found – trying our best to keep this family in the city as they have been in for nearing one year but feel we will lose them if marital troubles are not straightened out – called PA to search for Donna through residential school at reserve.

The incident was an interesting one. It was true that by white standards the suite was too small even for one family as large as the Beavers; but Indian people do not mind living close together. It even appears that the tenants were actually paying, an unusual situation indeed. When the landlord threatened the family with eviction, the wife failed in her attempt to make ends meet. Suffering under this social and economic loss, as well as a personal snub, she simply left town, apparently to visit her other children. The husband was in a very bad situation, since there was no day care centre in Saskatoon where he could place the children.

The Placement Officer found himself in the midst of family affairs and was the arbitrator of relationships. His entry illustrates his extreme unwillingness, given his investment in time and money, to lose this family under any circumstances. Two weeks later, he happily reported that the wife had come home, and that the marital problems had been straightened out. But the family was still in pretty desperate financial circumstances. Because of bad weather, the husband had not worked for a week and would not be paid for another week; in the meantime, there were no groceries in the house. Moreover, the family difficulties had resulted in further financial drain – the husband had taken to drink and promptly been fined $75 for consuming alcohol in a car. According to the Placement Officer, the fine was unfortunate; the

142

husband was not considered a drinking man, and had run afoul of the law because his Indian friends had been reckless.

His chief hope centred on low-rental housing, which the family had been promised by the end of the month. If he could tide them over with groceries and counselling until he got them established in their new home out of the West Side, the new surroundings would offer an incentive for better budgeting and a tighter family life. Indeed, the family situation was of the greatest concern to the Placement Officer. If it did not at least resemble a tight nuclear unit, it would not be possible for the family to qualify for low-rental housing. Therefore, every effort was made to impress upon the couple the necessity to get along and to keep relatives and boarders out of the house until they had obtained their low-rental living quarters.

At the end of the month, however, the Placement Officer noted with regret that his efforts to get the family new housing had been abortive:

Lost low-rental home due to inability to produce the $50.00 damage deposit – Dahl Agencies phoned them on Monday October 28/68 for deposit (as we had instructed subject to pay their office on Saturday Oct. 26) – subject told Dahl he didn't have the $50.00 but would have it later in the week – also told them that he quit his job – when Dahl heard this they immediately put on the brakes, thinking that, with a bad start like this, what would happen in the coming months – phoned subject and found the reason he had quit was that because he had two weeks pays plus holiday pay held back thought if he terminated employment he would get this and be able to .pay the $50.00 – talked him out of this misguided idea and he went back to work the next day, the 29th – cleared the air with Dahl (hopefully) – and they state that they have another home coming up on November 15th which they will assign to the Beaver family providing they produce the $50.00 – counselled subjects at length – told them I felt they hadn't been holding up their end of things – Mrs. Beaver has been drinking and they have been spending their money unwisely (they had plenty of warning to have the $50.00 ready) – Mrs. Beaver very shook up and said they would mend their ways – discussed with Mr. Timberg (Placement Officer in Regina) and we agree it would be a pity to lose the family after such a long attempt – we will pay the first

143

month's rent in low-rental accommodation if and when attained – believe this exercise has proved invaluable in pointing out the difficulty of successfully relocating a general labour applicant with a large family (even though the complete family has not as yet joined them).

In spite of appearances, the Beaver family had achieved a very enviable position. Family success had become indispensable to the local reputation of the Placement Officer; continued assistance was certain. All things, however, have a price. With the spiralling vested interest of the official in the survival of the Indian family, the missionary character of the relationship became complete. In the modulated civil-service voice of the Placement Officer: "they are like children. They need our assistance, it will take time for them to change."

The housing breakthrough came in November, when the family obtained a low-rental duplex with four bedrooms in a good white neighbourhood. The Saskatoon Local Housing Authority apparently had been re-assured by the IAB that the family was now a good risk. By this time, the husband had ready the $50 for a deposit, but could not come up with the first month's rent.[11] The entry into the file on November 25, 1968 is worth noting:

Saskatoon Local Housing Authority has finally accepted this family for low-rental duplex in Nutana – this is a breakthrough for us and we are watching developments very closely – subject paid $50.00 damage deposit and requested assistance with first month's rent – okayed this as it had already been discussed with Mr. Wolmark – subject will need furniture to move into this four bedroom accommodation and I've advised that we would have to clear this with Regina first – in view of the fact that we have spent quite a bit of time and funds with this family and that we have finally found new accommodation for them, it is recommended that we assist with the necessary furniture. If you will refer to Form 116 March 4/68 we indicated that more furniture would be needed when better accommodation was located . . . would you please advise immediately if it is okay to go ahead with the purchase of additional furniture – please bear in mind that this family is moving to brand new accommodations in a new

144

development and adequate furniture is a must if they are to adjust socially and otherwise.[12]

In fact, the Placement Officer had skilfully prepared for the furniture authorization, and was able to clear it officially with the provincial office in Regina three days after his letter of November 26. When the wife picked out a $25.00 chesterfield, he advised against buying cheap furniture: "it was very scruffy looking and would have been out of place in the new accommodation."

Once the family was in the new area, the counselling process was extended to include the Placement Officer's wife. She was to introduce the family to the white neighbourhood and to draw them into local organizations. Prior to the move to the low-cost housing development, the Placement Officer's wife had not met them, for they lived on the wicked West Side. Once out of that dreaded area, the Indians were acceptable for contact.

Have had long chats with Mrs. Beaver, she is quite frightened about the area she is moving to but believe I have allayed most of her fears – when the move is made I and wife will call on them to try to help them in their adjustment. Mrs. Beaver is so happy that she is speechless – she didn't ever think it could happen to her family and she is now looking forward to next June when she will bring in the rest of the children – arranged with Sask. Power to wait until next payday when subject would pay $15.00 deposit on meter – total expenditure on this family has been approximately $900.00 since March 1968 – future looks good for them at present and believe they will make the grade – it's a long hard road for a general labourer with a large family and if this family succeeds it will be a real accomplishment and most certainly encouraging for others who are better equipped but undecided.

It had also been a "long hard road" for the Placement Officer, and he communicated his sense of accomplishment to his colleagues and friends. He bubbled around the office, noting progress made and possibilities for the future. It had been a personal triumph for him, and his sense of accomplishment was reinforced by the gratification derived from a continuing paternalistic connection with the family. "They are slowly letting go of my hand but are taking the other one in friendship, which is satisfying." The attempts made to integrate the family into the local white community, however, did not go well. An entry in February noted:

> Had a phone call from a Mrs. Degras today inquiring if there were any Indian women in town who were lonesome, etc. and who would be interested in coming to the Thursday morning sessions called "Morning Fun for Women." To preclude any misunderstanding arising from the name of the club, it is a group of women (sponsored by the Zion United Church) who meet every Thursday morning to discuss shopping, decorating, child care, in fact any interesting topic. They felt an Indian woman would gain much from meeting other women and they also would gain from listening to her. Mrs. Degras sounds very sensible and realizes that people from other races must be treated as equals. I called Mrs. Beaver about this and suggested that such a club would be interesting and advantageous to her – she agreed and Mrs. Degras will be contacting her today. This is the type of orientation we have been hoping to find and we will follow it up closely to assess the impact it has on this family.

However, there were no further entries regarding "Morning Fun for Women." The wife was not interested in joining white neighbourhood associations of this kind. She went once, did not open her mouth, and never returned. Thus the attempt to bring the family into secondary associations in the suburbs failed.

This relatively minor failure was quickly overshadowed by a series of nearly catastrophic events following close upon the arrival in the new duplex and the accompanying vaulting hopes. First, there were employment problems. Western Pipeline, the employer of the husband, could not offer him a position until the middle of February; he could expect his first check sometime in March. Unemployment insurance contributed only $76 every two weeks, too small a sum to cover bills. The Placement Officer advised the husband to seek assistance from the Department of Social Welfare.

Secondly, the wife became pregnant with her eighth child, upsetting the delicate equilibrium of the marriage relationship. In the earliest months, she seems to have been attracted by the new house. The Placement Officer's wife gave assistance on shopping, budgeting and handling kitchen equipment, advice which was in fact needed. For example, the wife could not understand why the family refused to eat the meat she cooked. It turned out that she had been setting the oven at 500°. A short lesson cleared up the difficulty. The Placement Officer had also arranged some work for the wife – making mocassins for a local handicraft shop. It is difficult to know how much money was earned from this part-time work, but it obviously was helpful in the rather bleak financial circumstances of mid-winter. The wife saw to it that there was no drinking, that payments were being made as far as possible, and that family morale remained high. The birth of the new child, however, occasioned a crisis.

First, after February 17, it was necessary to seek more assistance from the Indian Affairs Branch to prepare for the baby; needed were money for groceries, rent, utilities ($70), and a babysitter while the wife was in the hospital with the child. Also, cost of drugs throughout the pregnancy had been high relative to total income, and the Placement Officer had to intervene with the Department of Social Welfare to have these taken care of. He was so concerned about the stability of "his" family that he authorized assistance for the purchase of an old car to provide better transportation to and from the work site for the husband. He assured the family that it would qualify for up-grading in the next year through the Extension Department of the University of Saskatchewan. Nonetheless, a deluge of familiar problems came with the baby. Sadness and dejection mark the entry for June 9:

Subject missed work on May 27th and 28th – wife was in hospital having a baby and their babysitter took off – when Mrs. Beaver returned home subject took off for Loon Lake intending to come back on June 2nd, wife very upset and said she wouldn't let him in if he came back – called Mr. E. Jasper, Meadow Lake, who investigated and said subject was on his way back (June 2nd) – didn't return until Friday – –in the meantime had two or three counselling sessions with wife who was determined to stay in the city – talked to subject on June 7th and he said his car broke down and he didn't have the money to fix it – finally got it fixed with help from Indian Affairs (Jacob Wingate who went to Loon Lake at our request) – back on the job this morning which we managed to have held for him but this has thrown the family back into the red – their gas was shut off and wife had no groceries – subject claims he left her money but she says no – who to believe? – in any event we don't want to see two years' work go down the drain and are happy to report that the couple has been reconciled and wife promises to do much better – believe she has been hard on John and he probably took off for a weekend through frustration and loneliness – guaranteed payment of a cab to take Mrs. Beaver to hospital and am including that amount here – hope they will manage to pay off groceries and gas account which we backed.

One important result of the incident was the further undermining of the job credibility of the husband. Two months later he was laid off with no early expectation of work. Another round of IAB assistance and reliance on the Department of Social Welfare was necessary. The Placement Officer felt compelled to justify the additional aid with the comment that "the amount spent on this family while relocating in the city this fiscal year is trivial as compared to the cost if they decided to return home [the reserve] and become welfare recipients." As indicated previously, however, there was much more involved in his decision to back the family – the maintenance of his own credibility.

The family spent the next two months, August and September 1969, on welfare, but now both husband and wife began drinking. Although the latter had indulged now and again on the reserve, the former apparently had had no serious problem with alcohol despite the offense of the previous year. The Welfare workers insisted on an AA course for both husband and wife, an experience which they both apparently enjoyed. By the time the husband went back to work on September 30, the drinking problem had been at least temporarily overcome. As a reward, the Placement Officer authorized the purchase of an electric clothes dryer for the family, with the argument that a family of that size required further labour-saving equipment in the home.[13]

Alas, recently after the husband returned to work, he was caught in a cave-in and sent home on crutches for six weeks (with compensation). In addition, marital problems surfaced once more.

The Placement Officer long maintained that the learning process was of great value, and that the family was advancing socially and economically despite their trials and tribulations. Other IAB officials had bets the other way. In the end, two years later, he realized he had lost: the family showed no visible sign of improvement. It would need intensive counselling and assistance in the foreseeable future.

Some families who have entered into this type of relationship have had greater success. One Indian from a Northern reserve, after placing complete faith in his Placement Officer for three years, has obtained off-reserve housing, and is now participating in the new Friendship Centre. Having stayed at the job for three years, and having married an Indian secretary who is also regularly employed, the husband is the pride of his Placement Officer. Still others have left the city for the reserve, unable to cope with urban problems despite special treatment.

In general however, the Beaver family is typical of the *Anomic* who have been assisted. Only a few can hope to qualify for off-reserve housing. Only a few can expect to be accepted by the *Affluent* unless they have shown beyond question that they have broken with their reserve grouping. In order to do this, they must withstand the test of survival in the urban environment by themselves.

In its effort to ensure that survival, the strategy of the "symbiotic relationship" is clearly inadequate in several respects. First, although it is the only approach to this group beyond welfare services sanctioned by the IAB, there is neither time nor money available for its implementation on a large scale. As of August 1969, only 109 relocation grants had been approved for the entire province of Saskatchewan, only 34 for the city of Saskatoon.[14] The Beaver family overcame many difficulties through the intervention of the Placement Officer. While he assisted this unit to which he was committed, however, many equally needy families failed to adapt. Special treatment cannot apply to more than a few families; it is therefore no major solution to problems arising from the urbanization of Indians and Metis.

Second, the "symbiotic relationship" deals with only one dimension of the total problem facing this group in the city. The Placement Officer has access to welfare and welfare-type patronage, but he can also lobby for larger benefits, such as relocation grants and, in exceptional cases, off-reserve housing. It is fair to say that the Placement Officer overcompensates for the educational and skill deficiencies of his clients in the employment and housing fields. The social and psychological dimensions of the problem, however, cannot be adequately covered within the confines of the present strategy. It is premised on docility and paternalism. The families who have obtained off-reserve housing defer totally to the Placement Officer; it cannot be otherwise – the power equation rewards the most servile.

The case studies reveal that, in an age of revival of consciousness, the paternalistic relationship, *as an essential ingredient of adaptive poverty programs,* cannot offer a framework within which an urban Indian identity can be generated. It also cannot offer a satisfactory replacement for the kinship relations that the *Anomic* Indians must curtail. Essentially, the "symbiotic relationship" is an adaptation of a nineteenth-century posture, in which it was assumed that "Indianness" would disappear. Although they are in great need, the *Anomic* Indians are in general unwilling to accept a strategy of assimilation which entails a total loss of their heritage and a humiliating subjection to an IAB Placement Officer. Instead they desire consultation and control, and the possibility of exploring and interpreting their position in the city through social action. That is precisely why the Friendship Centre concept is inadequate for this group of people: as the prerequisite for Government financing, it rules out social action from the start. Any suggestion of programs that would promote community power in the urban environment is given short shrift as encouraging "ghettoes" and racism.[15] The failure of the strategy of bureaucratic services and assimilation for the *Anomic* is certain and complete.

## Conclusion: Downward Mobility – the Perpetuation of the Poverty Cycle

The available evidence suggests that the present programs have attracted many people into the city from the reserves and the North, but have failed to prevent the growth of serious slum conditions. Even if one assumes that the large number of the "confirmed indigent" could hardly fail to present serious problems for the adaptation of migrants, the present strategy does not meet the needs of those people who desire upward mobility.

The present approach to the *Anomic* Indians and Metis is most unsatisfactory from the social and psychological points of view. It does not recognize the uniqueness of the Indian-Metis minority in an urban setting; it shows no sensitivity to the dynamics of the ethnic stratification system and the ideological demands of the cultural revival. The few cases of successful upward-mobility among the *Anomic* are merely isolated exceptions to the general rule of failure. From the historical perspec-

150

tive, it is quite clear that paternalism, at best, can foster only a small clientele, cut off from the other Indians and forced to rely for their survival on a close association with the Indian Affairs Branch. Only forms of activity that recognize the cultural tradition and that integrate activities into a vision of the future can nurture an adequate sense of identity. Similarly, a paternal relationship with white Placement Officers is no substitute for family and community associational patterns that provide mutual support in the crisis of modernization. The economic dimension is dealt with in as satisfactory a fashion as might be expected, given the educational and skill levels of the Indians in this grouping. Unfortunately this compensation is not enough to prevent failure and downward mobility in the vast majority of cases.

---

[1] Department of Indian Affairs and Northern Development, Indian Affairs Branch, *Summary Statement: Indian Families Receiving Relocation Services, 1966-1968*, and *Indian Families Receiving Relocation Services Other than Financial under Branch Services, 1966-1968*, Regional Office, Regina, Saskatchewan, 1969.

[2] Department of Indian Affairs and Northern Development, Indian Affairs Branch, *Memorandum Re: Assistance to Purchase Furniture and Household Equipment*, June 17, 1969, Regional Office, Regina, Saskatchewan. The present study was concluded at that date.

[3] A manpower survey of 5 agencies showed the average educational level in the Files Hills-Qu'Appelle Agency to be 8.08, as opposed to 6.93 for Touchwood, 7.02 for Crooked Lake, 6.68 for Battleford, and 6.00 for Carleton. Department of Indian Affairs and Northern Development, Indian Affairs Branch, *Education-Manpower Survey*, March 31, 1969.

[4] IAB and IMB *Placement Officer Reports*, 1967-1969. Compare with a provincial government statement that, of 788 native people placed between April and September 30, 1966, 16 per cent had remained on the job, 68 per cent had resigned, and 7 per cent had been dismissed. The average tenure of employment for those leaving work was seven weeks. Saskatchewan, Department of Natural Resources, *Annual Report*, 1967, p. 38.

[5] *Saskatoon Star-Phoenix*, March 26, 1970; April 1, 1970.

[6] *Education-Manpower Survey*, March 31, 1969; M. Shimpo and R. Williamson, *The Socio-Cultural Disintegration of the Fringe Saulteaux*, Centre for Community Studies, University of Saskatchewan, Saskatoon, 1965; *Salvation Army Files*, 1958-1969.

[7] *Salvation Army Files*, 1958-1969.

[8] *IAB Placement Officer Reports*. The Saskatchewan Task Force on Education did not carry out a follow-up study to see whether the newly-acquired skills were being employed. Saskatchewan Task Force on Education, *Indian and Metis Education Services in Saskatchewan, Reference Paper No. 3*, May, 1969, p. 21.

[9] Indian Affairs Branch, *Assistance to Purchase Furniture and Household Equipment, op. cit.* The figure is obtained by subtracting the number of off-reserve housing grants from the 34 relocation grants to the city (as of August, 1969).

[10] *IAB Placement Officer Reports.* Succeeding entries will not be indicated.

[11] The Saskatoon Local Housing Authority had made a considerable exception to its usual rule. In a conversation with the local representative, he indicated that, although Indians and Metis are not discriminated against in the low-rental area, they lack the one essential prerequisite, namely credit. Therefore, according to this man, very few families are accepted by the Local Housing Authority. He indicated that there were ten to twelve native families living there, and that these had regular employment with established agencies such as the Department of Social Welfare and others; *i.e.*, agencies which would attract the more reliable young Indians (Mr. Jones, Dahl Real Estate, *Interview,* October 5, 1969).

[12] *IAB Placement Officer Reports.*

[13] A good case could be made for the argument that the wife needed the dryer to survive, for along with the new addition, the other five children had joined the parents in Saskatoon.

[14] Indian Affairs Branch, *Assistance to Purchase Furniture and Household Equipment, op. cit.*

[15] Currie, *op. cit.,* p. 16.

# 8

## Leaders Without Followers:
## The Dilemma of Urban Indian
## Organizations

Without exception, the native organizations in Saskatoon have enjoyed a singular lack of broad support among the Indians and Metis themselves; but there is never a shortage of "leaders" willing to head yet another fragmented and ephemeral group. The results have been the same in every case; whether promoting bureaucratically-oriented self-help associations such as the Friendship Centre, or radical social action groups such as the Metis Society, the leaders quickly find themselves without followers.

Concerned Indians and whites, therefore, are confronted by a serious dilemma. In the Canadian political system, the most important single mechanism for influencing governmental decisions is organizational strength. Positive governmental action, on terms deemed acceptable by the Indians and Metis, is directly related to the articulation and aggregation of demands which would be politically costly to ignore. Only native leaders can develop these organizations, for the thrust of Indian consciousness is that they alone can speak for the Indian community in the cities or on the reserves. However, urban organizations have so little coherence that the "leaders" can hardly claim them to be representative of their ethnic group. The native minority in the city lacks a basic tool to ensure meaningful governmental concern.[2]

"Who speaks for the Indians?" is as frequently heard in Canada as "Who speaks for the Negroes?" is in the United States. The native people have as much difficulty in answering as do their black counterparts to the south. In fact, the women of Caucasian ancestry who staff the Extension Department of the University of Saskatchewan claim to be more genuine spokesmen for the natives than the "red power people." One lady claimed

153

that she was more "Indian" than a noted Metis radical and professor at the University of Saskatchewan.[3]

Not a few white IAB officials have expressed the same sentiment, although confidentially. The placement and counselling officers in particular claim to have far greater "meaningful" contact with the ordinary Indian than does the indigenous leadership. They have the "interests of the genuine Indian at heart, while the action-oriented leaders care only about their reputations."

The Indian and Metis leadership privately agree that their organizations are not reaching the Indian masses. No one speaks for them but themselves; they have chosen not to speak to the organizations which supposedly represent them, or, for that matter, to any other. The socio-political involvement of the poor Indian and Metis in urban programs is as yet nominal.

## Patterns of Community Decision-Making

Interestingly enough, despite the small number of native people involved in the organizations, there are identifiable factions within the leadership.[4] A first, highly acculturated group endorses a "debate" or "problem-solving" approach, maintaining that the stresses and strains of acculturation will eventually be resolved through rational discussion and practical reform. There is little opposition among the members of this group to the basic design of present programs, although they continually say that "we should make it easier for the Indians in the city." In any case, the stakes are not considered high enough to make trouble with the IAB. As might be expected, a large percentage of this group works for the IAB and thus implicitly endorses a policy of assimilation in the city.

Most members of this group would like to lose their Indian and Metis identity; they are probably the only Indians in Saskatchewan who favour the termination policy of the federal Government. Indeed, when they suffer discrimination – and the occasional blatant incident reminds them that they are not yet full citizens – they blame the *Indian Act* rather than "white society" or "racism." The victim of the worst known incident of housing discrimination in Saskatoon firmly believed that it was caused by "special status," and that the *New Policy* would put an end to such injustices.[5]

One of the most noteworthy characteristics of this group is its apparent appreciation of white society. Not only are "white" habits such as hard work, individualism and thrift accepted as governing norms, but the history of Indian administration is by no means given a blanket condemnation:

> There are two sides to everything. The Government tried to help the Indians, but they won't do anything. As soon as hand-outs began, the Indians began to drink rather than work. Now they are too lazy to work, and drink away everything that the Government gives them.[6]

The individuals who promote this strategy limit their organizational work to non-political self-help groups such as sewing clubs and Friendship Centres. Even here, they will not tolerate "radical talk." Since these groups are sponsored by the official agencies, no personal risk is involved. Meanwhile, such bodies promote the quiet adjustment of the Indians and Metis to city life.

A second posture is a "fight" or radical group pressure strategy. This group's fundamental premise is the existence of a basic difference between the native people and the larger society; the values and goals of the two sides are deeply opposed and cannot be reconciled within present socio-political forms.

> You cannot come to any conclusion but that it is a white supremacy society. And this would be true of all western civilization. They are very definitely white supremacist. So that rules out the possibility of us becoming integrated or assimilated ... therefore we have to accept that we are outside of it.[7]

Tactics call for the mobilization of a politicized native population, the use of group pressure and demonstrations, together with the threat of force, to elicit responses to their demands. One leader banks on the population explosion among the native population: "There are 70,000 of us [in the province] and we are growing twice as fast as the white population."[8] Friendship Centres are denounced as part of the "system." The Metis Society, for example, headed by Howard Adams, is not opposed to concessions, but it insists that these cannot disguise the incompatibility of interests resulting from the colonial experience in Canada. Moreover, concession-mongering is always done in terms of, and for the purpose of, politicization. At every occasion, the assumed savagery of colonial experience and the continuing discrimination against Indians and Metis in the province are drummed into listeners of all backgrounds.

A third posture group attempts to mediate between the two extreme positions. It accepts the premise that the native population forms an unassimilable group inside the larger society. On the other hand, it also believes that, given pragmatic adjustments, "radical incrementalism" so to speak, the values and goals of both sides can contribute to a mutually enriched society. It aims, therefore, at something beyond the Friendship Centre concept, but it does not believe that a strategy of confrontation is either practicable or theoretically sound. Instead, it relies on persuasion and bargaining for the alleviation of specific grievances.

The organization in Saskatoon which best expressed this strategy was the Saskatoon Indian Committee (SIC), formed by a small number of Indian families in the autumn of 1967 to press for the honouring by the Government of so-called "treaty rights." Indian law is still in its infancy in Canada, and the specific legal position of Indians living off the reserve is not clear. The Saskatoon Indian Committee was determined that medical and dental expenses as well as school supplies would remain covered by the Indian Affairs Branch. These are highly important issues, involving large sums of money. The medicare issue had recently aroused great controversy when a provincial magistrate ruled that *Treaty Six* entitled all Indians to free medicare. *Treaty Six,* alone among the treaties, had stated that "a medicine chest shall be kept at the house of each Indian agent for the use and benefit of the Indians at the direction of such agent."[9] SIC felt it urgent to inquire further into the matter, since there were indications that the IAB did not feel itself bound by either *Treaty Six* or the recent decision. Similarly, in September 1967, the local IAB office had dragged its feet on the payment of school supplies to Indian families. In response, the families concerned met, established an organization with a president and secretary, and fired off letters to provincial and federal legislators. To their surprise, they found a great deal of support among the politicians. The immediate demands were satisfied and they decided to meet regularly as a permanent organization in order to exert group pressure as important issues arose. Another characteristic marked it off from the other groups such as the Friendship Centre – SIC was composed only of native people; whites were not allowed even to attend the meetings as advisors. Moreover, it owed nothing to the official agencies or white voluntary groups.

The fledgling organization found itself groping toward a concept, a concept of social action midway between two extremes.

What is apparent here is the appearance of a typology of community decision-making described by a number of authors (although always using different terms) to order various forms of community conflict resolution.[10] R. M. Kramer, in an excellent study of community power politics during the American "war on poverty," also noticed what he termed "the convergence among attempts to order the basic prophecies by which change in community policies can be accomplished."

> The preceding analysis and interpretation can be a source of hypothesis and contribute to emergent theories of community decision-making, conflict resolution and planned change. There seems to be a considerable overlap between these concepts, and they probably refer to the same social processes but from different perspectives. For example, the pattern of community responses to the pressures to maximize the participation of the poor that has been classified as a debate, game or fight is quite similar to a typology of 'purposes, social change at the community level' recently proposed by Rowland L. Warren. This scheme is based on a continuum of consensus-difference-dissension, which implies either collaborative, campaign, or contest strategies respectively. These in turn are virtually equivalent to a classification of methods of resolving organizational conflict suggested by March and Simon: problem-solving; education; persuasion and bargaining; and pressure.[11]

Kramer goes on to suggest that the pattern of power and the coalition capability[12] of the ethnic community influences the degree of opposition or agreement. For example, if a group can mobilize little power, the likelihood of a strategy of debate is high: the higher the power concentration, the greater the possibility of dissension and conflict.

But in the case of the urban Indians and Metis in Saskatoon, no such patterns emerge. It is not possible to link the strategies of the various groups such as power distribution and community size. In the Saskatoon case, none of the strategies outlined – debate, game, fight – find support among the rank and file Indians and Metis. While the native population of "objectively oppressed" people numbers over two thousand, all the excitement

157

and fuss over organizational strategy goes on inside a group of about thirty families.

All writers on the subject agree that formal Indian organizations are exceedingly weak, and that only a small percentage of Indians and Metis are in close touch with these activities. Thus Joan Ablon:

> The reality of an actual Indian community is indeed tenuous when considered in the perspective of the total population in the area, notwithstanding the number and frequency of activities sponsored by Indian organizations. Less than one-sixth of the adult Indians are effectively touched by these activities. Probably not more than thirty adults are regularly active in more than any one club.... Characteristic of the operation of these groups are a lack of authoritarian leadership, a general practice of group participation in planning, and a frequent absence of concrete pre-event duty assignment (with much complaining afterward about the often resulting confusion).[13]

Also:

> Most families limited their formal social interaction to attendance at only the largest Indian events such as Christmas parties, the annual Indian Day picnic, or more rarely a Four Winds dance or pow-wow.[14]

From his Los Angeles study, Price concluded that: although formal Indian associations (athletic clubs, churches, clubs and centres) have extensive mailing lists of nominal members, only about 20 per cent of Los Angeles Indians are active in such associations."[15]

Thus far, the programs offered by native organizations in Saskatoon have not appealed, or been accessible, to the *Anomic* or *Welfare* groupings. The group of actual participants is so small, and each member knows everyone else so well, that the differing social and political attitudes are almost necessarily cast in the framework of biographical analysis or small group theory. The one relatively consistent thread is the unwillingness of the IAB or IMB native officials to get involved in radical groups.

At the same time, Indian organizations continue to proliferate; the minority of organizers exhibit zeal at the very least. In

Saskatoon, the Saskatoon Indian Committee, the Indian and Metis Development Society, the Friendship Centre, and the Metis Society were all formed within one year. Obviously some interests must be involved in this constant round of organizing. Three questions are raised. 1) What are the chief sources of weakness of Indian urban groups? 2) What functions do organizations fulfil for the leadership? 3) How are these related specifically to their inability to attract a mass following in the cities?

## Sources of Weakness of Indian Organizations

*Diverse Origins.* A first, and obvious, problem facing native urban organizations is the difficulty of uniting individuals from the diverse Indian and Metis communities in the province. These are anything but homogeneous, differing widely in tribal origin, language and treaty area. The employment records in Saskatoon show a majority of Cree in the city, but there are also Ojibway, Saulteaux, Sioux, Assiniboin and Chipewyan. Indians are invariably precise about their tribal and reserve origins. Throughout most of their life as an administered people, they have identified themselves with parochial units at the expense of any strong feelings of national identity or thoughts about collective action. There are also important differences in the type and degree of white contact. Finally, the legal and administrative distinction between Indians and Metis greatly inhibits collective action by the two groups. The reserve history has, in many cases, added to the hostility between essentially the same blood groups, particularly in those areas where the Metis fared better than the Indians.[16] In the North, on the other hand, the Metis are despised as being worse off than the Indians. There are, in short, formidable problems of diversity to be overcome.

*Dependence on Official Agencies*

*Finances.* Unless an urban organization can muster support from some powerful body or group, it cannot master the problem of finances. The Indians and Metis in the city do not have an independent source of funds sufficient to finance an effective organization. In practice, this means that they must convince a Government agency at the municipal, provincial or federal level that their project is worthy of its support. The process of Government is slow, and taxpayers want a guarantee that their money is carefully audited (if not well invested). In practice, autonomy under these circumstances is only a remote possibility.

As we have seen, the indirect hostility of the IAB toward self-help projects gives it an obvious bias in the type of project it selects for assistance. For example, although it refused to contribute to the Big Bear Gallery, it enthusiastically supported an almost identical project because the Treasurer would be an IAB official.

*Information.* Local government officials have at their disposal a great deal of information which is essential for effective organization in the urban environment. Some of this is in fact confidential, and it is wise not to distribute it. At the same time, there is a wide range of data that could very easily be given over to a local group seeking information about residents and the nature and origins of the native people in the City of Saskatoon. A great variety of skills are required to elicit this information from the officials of the Indian Affairs Branch and the Indian-Metis Branch, as well as from those of the Salvation Army, Catholic Family Services, etc. The only certain method is to provoke one agency to compete against another in a show of friendship toward a project. This is particularly the case with the Indian Affairs Branch and the Indian-Metis Branch, the two most important agencies which use information as a weapon against local groups. Flattery is also an important tool, but few people, white or Indian, have a well-developed capacity for self-mortification. It is very unlikely in any case that a native person could obtain this information, given the present staffing of the official agencies. It does not help that the more *Affluent* Indians and Metis are being employed – they tend to be more suspicious of the native population than the white administrators.

*The Bureaucratic "Vanishing Act."* The intense bureaucratic tangle encountered in the official agencies victimizes fledgling native organizations. Interviews with IAB and IMB officials, well acquainted with the jargon of community development, can easily convince the uninitiated that every possible self-help program has already become operational or is "in the works." It is not immediately clear that this apparent pre-empting of any organizational rationale is a product of semantics. The heavy prose of introductory sociology textbooks has been mastered by the local officials. After a great deal of exploration – which costs time and money – it becomes clear that there are few plans, that almost nothing has been accomplished where plans have been implemented, and that no agency has a clear view of the situation. The bureaucratic maze is intimidating; there is a great temptation to admit that the agencies can in fact do everything better than a native institution, despite the overwhelming evidence of their inefficiency.

*Co-opting the Leadership.* The various levels of Government have at their disposal a decisive weapon for fragmenting the leadership of an Indian or Metis organization: they can hire them at lucrative salaries. Native organizations are desperately in need of the kind of talent that can plow through the many obstacles which confront them – people with ability, determination and technical competence. Should a local organization manage to find such a person – and there are very few in all of Saskatchewan – it is almost inevitable that either the Indian Affairs Branch or the Indian-Metis Branch will recruit him. Given the salary and career opportunity, it is difficult for the native person in question to reject the offer.

In 1966, Premier W. Ross Thatcher indicated that he was ready to employ every Indian in Saskatchewan with a high school diploma, thereby preventing even the possibility of their recruitment by independent native organizations in the cities or the countryside. In his opinion, "this is just one more step in giving the Indians a say in Government business."[17] The view of the Premier is consistent with the official line that the participation of the Indian and Metis is provided through employment, rather than organizational self-help and social action programs.

The strategy of co-opting means that most of the native organizers at the moment are now, or will be in the near future, members of the government bureaucracies. There is one advantage: money is more likely for the projects in which IAB or IMB employees are directly involved. But the disadvantage is savage. The IAB has definite preferences – for Friendship Centres, for example. Although the Saskatoon Friendship Centre was only a name in 1969, it received a grant on the assurance that the proper Indians would be on its Board of Directors. Self-help projects are greatly jeopardized.

*Co-opting the Radical Leadership.* If the official agencies co-opt the moderates, the ever-resourceful Canadian society manages to disarm the radicals. The University fulfils an especially valuable role here. White would-be intellectuals are relieved to believe that they have been powerful and wicked in the past, and enjoy being constantly reminded of their guilt. It greatly eases their present sense of futility and powerlessness. At the same time, it flatters the native radicals to have an audience so sympathetic and so utterly uncritical. With the growth in popularity of radical groups on the left, this white audience has become very large.

It is unlikely that the native radicals involved see the danger of the connection. Dr. Howard Adams, the fiery Metis writer and University Professor and Director of the Metis Society in 1969, draws his main support in the province from the University rather than from native people. Probably in the short run this support is more effective politically, as long as the Government is not aware that the support among the native population is marginal. In any case, it does foster the illusion of a large devoted following. Dr. Adams' prose is too flowery and intellectual for the native people; it is geared to the young students who crowd into his meetings. What he fails to realize is that the whites will cease to believe when their immediate interests are threatened by a project. Even Big Bear Gallery lost its "Citizens' Committee" when it moved to the East Side of town, rather than remaining on the West Side outside the field of vision of local intellectuals and prosperous whites.

Even more seriously, the University is an integral part of the society that the radicals are condemning. It places men like Howard Adams or the young Indian radicals beyond the poverty-stricken native population. It opens possibilities for speaking tours, usually with lucrative returns. Invariably these arrangements are concluded with other paternalistic institutions, and usually funded by Government agencies – the same agencies, such as the Indian Affairs Branch, that are being condemned. Growing recognition in the country and the province adds to the invulnerability of the University connection; it usually leads to an escalation of radical demands and further myth-making. Thus, in the past year, Saskatchewan has become not merely the "Mississippi of the North," but also "Biafra." Books and other publications appear. Continued association with the white intellectuals is assured, but at the cost of a following among the native population.

Thus the ideal method of capturing the native leadership and rendering it impotent is to retard the leap from myth-making to myth-testing by institutionalizing the radical. The legend of an infinitely creative, productive, proud and beautiful people crushed under the ruthless oppression of an egotistical, money-oriented imperialism directed by Uncle Shylock will not survive a day's emergence in the intricacies of a subtle Saskatchewan colonialism. If it is allowed to blossom and bring forth ideological fruit, this vision is essentially the privilege of the well-off Indians who spawn minor reputations by repeating tales of personal woe and triumph. But the capacity for action is lost.

After a certain point, extreme radicalism among the Indian and Metis leadership becomes yet another subtle ploy by the cunning white man to break the connection between that leadership and their own people. It lures the radical leaders into a closer and closer communication with the white minority that finds ideological gratification in a frenzied negativism. At that level of native righteousness, there is no longer the capacity or will to sacrifice for an extremely underdeveloped native society in the cities and countryside.

## Ideological Constraints

The possibility of implementing organizational strategies is very much limited by surrounding ideological sensitivities. An urban Indian group cannot survive either a radical leadership or an overly-dominant white vanguard. The failure of the Saskatoon Indian Committee proved the former point; that of the Saskatoon Friendship Centre, the second.

Composed of a small group of relatively well-off Indian families in Saskatoon, the Saskatoon Indian Committee was a pressure group bargaining for specific legal rights. As indicated above, it touched on highly sensitive and technical ground. Needing technical assistance and yet very sensitive about white involvement, the SIC enlisted a radical, well-known Metis "spokesman." The SIC insisted that he was only that – a mouthpiece. According to its secretary, he was there only to help formulate demands and to compose letters. There were, however, at least two other reasons for this choice: first, by recruiting him, SIC tried to add to its own power base. Over-conscious of the small size of its membership, it felt that his prestige would broaden its appeal and its bargaining power. The choice thus revealed a continual restless search on the part of the native people to find a secure power base, erasing their extraordinary lack of initial advantage in a white society. Secondly, the Indians involved were flattered to invite him and to be his equal. Although a halfbreed, he was a university man; the first is a disadvantage; the latter, however, more than compensates. For the Metis leader on the other hand, association with actual Indians was a feather in

163

his cap, so to speak. He came into the radical fold as a middle-aged man, well after the movement was under way. This dubious past reinforces the natural cleavage between Treaty Indians and Metis, based on legal and administrative separation as well as an ingrained sense of superiority of the "full-blooded" Indian.

After the SIC met a warm reception from government officials, it sent a delegation to Regina to press the "medicine chest" issue; the Metis radical was a member of the group. This represented no inconsiderable breakthrough for him, but it became apparent very shortly that he and SIC were a heady mixture. In fact, it was inevitable that the former would become more than a mere "spokesman." Riding a wave of publicity, he was the person who presented suggestions during the meetings; the other members of the SIC tended to agree. He chaired; they followed. Not unnaturally, a radical is a radical, and he tried to swing the organization into radical paths. Messages of solidarity were sent out to other militant groups of Indians and Metis across the country. He pressed home the view that the SIC should be a politicizing agency, linked with similar organizations. Power, he felt, would increase with the overall increase in organizational strength. This view had been extolled by his white supporters, especially those who were entirely out of touch with the realities of Saskatchewan (including a curious couple from New Jersey). At the same time, less and less effort was devoted to the study of the actual intricate legal questions; as a result, the members showed a most shocking naïveté about judicial procedure in their communications with legislators.

Whatever the value of attempting to politicize the masses, the SIC had other things to do if it were to remain an effective political pressure group. The essential difference between the SIC people and their Metis spokesman was that they were Indians subject to the *Indian Act* and with specific grievances, while he was an intellectual with a secure job and assured status. As long as the SIC concentrated on giving a reasoned assessment of a specific situation, it had support among both government and opposition leaders. It did not have a broad base, and therefore had little power in an electoral sense, but no one cared to test its strength as long as it carefully informed the governmental process about native demands. Government legislators welcomed the articulation of these interests, and the political parties vied with each other in supporting them. There was no questioning the strategy initially adopted by the SIC; if there was hostility shown

164

toward it by the local Indian Affairs Branch office, there certainly was countervailing support from Regina and Ottawa. However, the character of the SIC was changed by the later emphasis on "radicalism and racism," combined with an absence of hard work on specific legal points. Confidence waned; letters remained unanswered. Sensing a slow-down, the Metis turned to the Metis Society and began to deal directly with the Government. As a bargaining group, the SIC was forgotten and disintegrated; the families involved still tend to associate together socially, but with considerable back-biting.

The other extreme – domination by a "provisional white vanguard" – was exhibited by the first abortive attempt to establish a Friendship Centre in Saskatoon. It started with a bang in the fall of 1967. There was an official opening with the Mayor in attendance, traditional costumes and a rather embarrassed burying of the hatchet.[18] Offices were obtained, although they were admittedly too small, and a mixed native-white board with an elaborate committee structure was set up. The Centre did not have a grant to begin with; rather, it was to receive one only after it was established and under way. At first tremendous support was shown, even by the native population. Huge crowds turned up for the initial meetings. The Centre's main task, however, was the drawing up of a program – otherwise it had to raise enough money to get along on its own, but this it did not have the capacity to do.

Instead of developing programs, the lady who dominated the organization lectured church groups and appealed for their support. She was intent on being the leader, but had no leadership ability. Lacking confidence, she turned to the white element in the directorship for support, but in the process lost that of the Indians. Chaos at first threatened, and then set in. The whites would not run the Centre completely because they were only transitional. The Indians intensified their dislike of their leading lady. Keys to the office began to proliferate, and articles were stolen. At last, in an indecorous finale, young couples registered regular sexual triumphs in the Union Building. It was, after all, a Friendship Centre. Eventually the offices were closed, and the more sedate postal workers moved in.

The permissible limits of white control (and ineffective white control at that) had been overreached. There was enthusiasm at first, and a large number of young people in from the Reserves in high school could very well have profited from recreational and counselling programs. But the Centre became identified with white supporters; it never became the Indians' project, and that was fatal.[19]

## Political Culture

The theory of "political culture" suggests another factor in the organizational weakness of Indian groups – the inability of Indians and Metis to deal pragmatically and effectively with problems in well-ordered and well-run meetings. According to this theory, Indians, due to their loosely-organized, undifferentiated social organizations, simply lack the collective discipline required to open and adjourn a meeting, to follow a previously prepared agenda, and to maintain order. Nothing is accomplished because no common action is being pursued.

Anyone familiar with Indian groups realizes the force of the argument. Meetings are extraordinary, with literally hours of silence at a stretch during which nobody dares to say a word, or with hours on end when everyone shouts abuse. Few Indians relish the thought of taking the responsibility for chairing a meeting.

Crisis situations in native organizations, such as the drafting of a brief, are usually dealt with by an appeal to white "resource persons." Invariably three stages are involved. First, the native organizers maintain that white experts have absolutely nothing to say in Indian affairs, and that only Indians know what to tell the Government. Second, they suggest that perhaps some advice would be acceptable, providing the whites take no part in the actual formulation of proposals. Finally, the whites end up writing the brief, and submitting it in the name of the relevant Indian organization.

However, all arguments resting heavily on the "political culture" idea tend to deal with symptoms rather than causes. All kinds of tests have shown that Indians do not have modernizing values.[20] Anthropologists have found that they do not press for rights and are not competitive.[21] But these are global findings, referring to broad cultural characteristics. In the Saskatoon experience, it was shown on numerous occasions that the *Affluent* Indians and Metis could command a high level of political skill *when it was worth their while to invest the time*. A political culture is redefined by each generation, which modifies a heritage under the impact of new situations and challenges.

In one case, for example, the Indians showed tremendous skill in bargaining for a grant from the provincial Government. Constant prodding was coupled with a very able wooing of the opposition. Visits were arranged and structured so as to give the impression of rather more support than the organization enjoyed in the larger community. Powerful support was mustered in the white community in an effort to present a broad united front to the Government. The argument can only be tested by looking at the reward system for the *Affluent*. It is essential that the motivations for organizing be explored.

### Rewards for the Affluent

*Local Prestige.* First, there is the incentive of local popularity. *Affluent* native people find themselves in a white society eager for news about the Indian. The white community demands a native leadership, and is prepared to extend publicity to the leaders of Indian and Metis organizations. Publicity, however, is not an end in itself, even though native people, like whites, have an infinite capacity for accepting flattery. Rather, recognition offers tangible rewards through connections with powerful groups, agencies and people. Indians are acutely aware of the power of influence, and brilliant in exploiting it. One Indian woman, active in organizations, has consistently lined up a formidable array of references when dealing with official agencies, *just in case* they should balk. By now, assisted by corridor chatter, she has great influence in these agencies.

If the rewards of local fame offer an incentive for organizing, the same logic yields a heavy competition for positions of leadership. A stable leadership would restrict the number of the *Affluent* who could get in the news and meet important people. An internal dynamic therefore encourages the sabotaging of existing organizations, and promotes a savage rivalry for the headship of new ones. An interesting illustration of this process is shown in the competition between the Indian and Metis Development Society and the Friendship Centre. As discussed above, the Big Bear Gallery was a non-profit organization, although associated with a self-employed Indian. Since the first attempt at a Friendship Centre had failed, and it was no longer in existence, the gallery developed the functions of a Friendship Centre. In fact, by the time the issue became acute – when the new Friendship Centre obtained a grant, although it had neither members nor directors – both organizations had little prestige in any camp, white or Indian. Obviously, the two should have joined forces rather than compete for members. Predictably, however, they did not:

> Asked if the Centre would join forces with a group operating Big Bear Gallery ... chairman of the board of directors said they could not amalgamate. The Gallery is a private enterprise interested in showing a profit, while the Centre is a non-profit project with different aims.[22]

What the "different aims" were was not made clear. They were still not explained even after the Centre had obtained a building of its own. In this sense, the director of the Gallery was correct in pointing out that "the Gallery is already used in that capacity [as a Friendship Centre] but it does not receive any Government grants for it." On the other hand, the competitive urge was too high to be resisted. Thus "his group was hoping to incorporate a Friendship Centre within the Gallery." In fact, several new people working for the official agencies desperately wanted a *new* Centre, and had the influence to obtain a grant. Whether the Centre survives will depend on the members of this group not falling out amongst themselves, with each one interested in a new program.

*Myth Making.* A second factor involved in urban native organizations refers to a psychological imperative. The urge to organize does not appear to be closely linked in many cases to clear *practical* objectives. More simply, a major function of organizations is not to promote action, but to liberate and politicize in a safe environment. Meetings are heavily ritualistic, with dreams and myths flying aimlessly about. The psychological dimension is best displayed by describing a series of meetings that eventually resulted in the creation of the Big Bear Gallery.

Informal weekly meetings began in a private apartment among a group of Indians and whites, with the objective of "finding out what the native people of Saskatoon wanted." No tape recorder was used; no notes were taken. These were prerequisites of mutual confidence. No persuasion was ever used to increase attendance; people were invited for "evenings," but these gatherings invariably lasted far into the night. They were always held at the same place, generally with drinks available if desired. However, they were always "talk and think" sessions. People broke up into small groups later at some meetings, but they were never parties. By February, the people who regularly attended these meetings realized that an organization existed. One Indian expressed the opinion of the group when he spoke of it as "something altogether different, with no vested interests, no political direction and no bad feelings."

Most of the white participants dropped out when it became clear that the Indians did not want a survey. The question of a social history had been raised, and to this they responded positively, but the native people felt that they had been over-surveyed, that surveys were a form of intolerable prying, and that they accomplished nothing. In fact, the white students and professionals involved *had* had academic papers in mind. The exodus of many left a small, committed group of them.

Greater amity, however, was not the result. Instead, the meetings entered a new phase of verbal violence. Again there was neither agenda nor chairman and no minutes were taken. The white people who remained were mercilessly attacked for their historical sins. Gradually it became clear that the hostility was a measure of native confidence in the white people at the meetings. Two months of association in a hospitable environment, where a great deal of mutual trust had been generated, had precipitated catharsis.

Verbal catharsis may well be the first step in the political regeneration of many Indian people. The violent denunciation of Indian Affairs, and a merciless and cruel indictment of white society, pricked the bubble that held the native people numb and repressed. Years of pent up anger boiled over into overt rage. The miserable history of the Conquest was recounted with a crude righteousness; all evils – disease, hunger and poverty – were ascribed to the whites. A sense of dignity and manhood was visibly restored. The function of the white people in the group was to elicit and encourage the catharsis. They sat back and took boundless and sometimes personal condemnation even though the insults were completely unfair. The verbal violence recreated the circumstances of the Conquest; the blind and impotent rage of the conquered was released on the descendants of the settlers, and then melted away.

With the psychological breakthrough, myths could be verbalized. The historical legends about a happier past, free from sickness and violence, full of cultural achievement, prior to the coming of the whites, could be given expression. The historical validity in this case, as in almost any case of a revived nationalism, is irrelevant. The function of "myth-making" was to bolster the confidence necessary to act.

Moreover, it created a great belief that things could be done. It appeared less hopeless to try to change an industrial society so intimidating in its power. The formidable organizational ability and resource control of the larger society undermine the confidence of native reformers; Canadian Indians are terrified to challenge white society in actual action programs.

Myth-making was an essential prerequisite for independent action. The interaction of the two ethnic groups had changed; they had participated in a decisive experience. Both sides had become aware of many unpleasant things about themselves, but the native participants especially no longer feared their thoughts and their fantasies.

However, action programs by definition transcend the realm of myth and fantasy. After myth-making comes the more difficult phase of "myth-testing." Actual projects force a confrontation with reality, and demand that the native people move matters and things. The transition from the first to the second phase is the crucial ingredient of institution-building. In the case of the Big Bear Gallery, the transition was very imperfect. When it came time for action, it became clear that the *Affluent* Indians were tied to the level of myth-making. Having met together for three months, they had achieved their objectives.

The sense of priority is shown by comparing the behaviour of the *Affluent* with that of the *Anomic* Indians who took part in the meetings. For the latter, the group experience had been equally important as an exercise in moral recovery, but unlike the *Affluent*, they wanted to implement the chosen objective – to set up a cultural centre where professional artists would give weekly instruction to Indians and Metis in the city. The hard work of cleaning and carpentry was done by these few people alone, while the *Affluent* disassociated themselves from action programs. Moreover, as soon as the Big Bear Gallery opened, they contributed to a hate campaign against it, putting even more of the work burden on the *Anomic*. A few of the latter continued to come into late summer, but the strain was too great for their resources. Although less bureaucratically-oriented and more inclined to sacrifice for a cause which they consider worthwhile, they lacked the leisure and the contacts of the *Affluent*.

## The Failure of the Affluent to Obtain a Mass Following

Were the Indians and Metis of Saskatoon able to cooperate, they would form a powerful pressure group. Yet the experience of the Big Bear Gallery, and it is only one example among many, suggests that the *Affluent* have little interest in assisting self-help projects that aim at a mass following.

First, there is little in the reserve heritage that would predispose the three groups to work together for a common objective. There is no basis for the belief that a common front would be possible, much less desirable, except for ceremonial occasions. The *Anomic* and *Welfare* have had bad experiences at the hands of the *Affluent* Indians as well as of the whites with whom they have had contact.

Second, the "welfare syndrome" gives the poor Indians and Metis a vested interest in keeping quiet. The slum dwellers have nothing to gain from antagonizing the powers that be, or from helping to undermine the bureaucracies and public benevolence which provide their dole. It is all well and good for the *Affluent* to say that welfare is harmful to the spirit. At the slum level, Indian identity does not depend on the puritan ethic. For the lowest class of native people, it pays to be quiet, to lie if necessary, and to establish a secretive identity based on tricking the white man out of minimal goods and services.

As for the intermediate group, the dependence on the bureaucracies is so great in the present system, that these families simply cannot afford to risk alienating their counsellors. The *Anomic* in Big Bear Gallery showed great courage in participating in a self-help project. If they cannot stand the paternalism, there is no alternative but to return to the reserve, for the Indian Affairs Branch and the Indian-Metis Branch have enormous powers of blackmail or coercion at their disposal in the community.[23]

There is the added difficulty of finding time and resources to attend meetings which are always badly chaired and often go on throughout the night. Babysitters are expensive and very hard to find. If the Indians have seasonal work, normally they are locked in a tight employment situation, and must be prompt and alert to obtain a permanent job out of it or to obtain good recommendations for another seasonal or permanent job. Moreover, a car is necessary to travel around the city, especially during the winter when meetings are usually held; but most of the intermediate families either do not own one, or they cannot afford to run it during the harsh Saskatchewan winter.

But more important than any of these reasons is the inability of the *Welfare* and *Anomic* to associate with families in the *Affluent* category. Feuds and memories divide the classes. The relative ease of the urbanization and the public recognition of the one grouping contrast with the savage difficulties of the others. On the one side there is self-righteousness; on the other, resentment.

Nor do the programs adopted or outlined by the organizers in the *Affluent* class touch the central problems facing the *Anomic* families that are struggling to survive. *Welfare* Indians can at least get coffee in the Friendship Centre and shoot a game of pool; but the intermediate or *Anomic* family needs more than coffee and a pool table, more even than school books and medicare. It needs everything. The *Anomic* family is a living crisis; not just one issue disturbs it – it is the totality of circumstances which conspire against its adaptation to city life. The culprit is the dualism which exists between it and the larger society. Everything is new and unfamiliar. Determined to be respected by the larger society and to adapt on its terms, although not to be assimilated, the *Anomic* Indian requires massive assistance. But from whom? His rising consciousness renders the forms of assistance of the official bureaucracies obsolete; yet he cannot expect enlightened leadership from the *Affluent* Indians from whom he is alienated. With their limited resources and leadership, Indian organizations cannot hope to match the admittedly low effectiveness of the governmental programs. In short, there is no form of participation recognized in the literature which is relevant to this total problem.

We can now see most clearly the difficulty with the Friendship Centre concept: it caters only to the *Affluent* and the *Welfare* Indians. Here the Centres do many good things. They provide experience in management for the *Affluent*, while they provide considerable assistance to poor Indians and Metis, guiding them to available social services, while giving them a place to stop for a sandwich or coffee. The Centres in Winnipeg and Toronto claim considerable success in helping people to adjust to city life while keeping them off the bottle.

In Toronto, for example, a Centre report claimed at least part of the credit for limiting the drop-out rate to less than 10 per cent in a group of sixty trainees. "There appears to be a desire to meet someone from your own surroundings, who can speak your own language."[24] A similar experience was reported in San Francisco: "Thus the formal groups often served to stabilize many wobbly new relocatees and allow them the security of an Indian meeting place and an opportunity to interact with others like themselves with the same problems as they adjusted to city life."[25] In the Saskatoon situation, this certainly is not the case. The *Affluent* Indians and Metis have no desire to mix with social rejects, Indians or non-Indians. The white beats who hang out at Friendship Centres associate them even more with Skid Row.

Essentially, the *Affluent* have already achieved so enviable a social position, relative to their reserve aspirations, that they have no incentive to put their futures on the line for the larger cause. For social and historical reasons, they have benefited from the "silent revolution" far more than their ethnic brothers. According to the *Hawthorn Report*, "the level of services not deemed appropriate for Indians is basically a spill-over of changed citizen-government relationships in White society."[26] The native organizations have done little even for the *Affluent*. If even *they* have not been materially rewarded by organizational power, why should they sacrifice for the poorer strata?

## Conclusion

There is little likelihood, with the present policy framework, that urban Indians and Metis will initiate and sustain organizations with a higher level of effectiveness than the Friendship Centres. The many linkages between the native social system and the larger society place a high premium on apathy among the *Welfare* and *Anomic*, and a carefully controlled rhetoric in the *Affluent* grouping. The common denominator is powerlessness. While the fringe benefits of Friendship Centres (and other organizations) cannot be dismissed as inconsequential, enthusiasm should not be allowed to obscure their inherent limitations. It is one thing to applaud the efforts of Indians and whites which have resulted in functioning groups; it is quite another to assume that they resolve the structural impediments to united action by a highly organized constituency.

¹ Students agree that Indian leadership has been practically nonexistent since the setting up of the reserves, where the political structure encouraged a passive acceptance of IAB directives. Until very recently, and in some cases even now, authority lay with the reserve agent and superintendent through whom grievances were channelled. The Chief and Councillors provided the functions of a ratifying body. They lacked political authority, were divorced from informational channels, and had to operate in defiance of traditional forms of association. There was, then, very little opportunity for the development of political skills. Glimmerings can be noted, however, on many reserves and there are promising signs in the provincial and regional organizations.

² For a good discussion of the problem, see *Hawthorn Report*, p. 364ff.

³ A strong scent of self-interest (and self-importance) is produced by expressions of white concern over "unrepresentative" native leaders.

⁴ The following discussion refers only to the cities.

⁵ *Hawthorn Report*, Appendix 3, pp. 381-397.

⁶ *Interview*, August 2, 1969.

⁷ "Political Profile: An Interview with Howard Adams, College of Education, University of Saskatchewan," *Saskatoon Commentator*, July 30, 1969.

⁸ *Saskatoon Star-Phoenix*, January 4, 1969.

⁹ Department of Citizenship and Immigration, Indian Affairs Branch, *Treaty Six*, Ottawa, 1961, p. 16.

¹⁰ Kramer, *op. cit.*, Rowland L. Warren, *Types of Purposive Social Change at the Community Level*, Brandeis University Papers in Social Welfare No. 11, Waltham, 1965; James G. March and Herbert A. Simon, *Organizations*, Wiley, New York, 1958, pp. 129-130.

¹¹ Kramer, *op. cit.*, p. 182.

¹² "Coalition capability": the capacity to organize and maintain an association of minority and allied groups that can mobilize appropriate and sufficient power to countervail the concentrated power already against them. *Ibid.*, p. 186.

¹³ Joan Ablon, "Relocated American Indians in the San Francisco Bay Area: Social Interaction and Indian Identity," *Human Organization*, Vol. 23, No. 4, (winter, 1964), pp. 299-300.

¹⁴ *Ibid.*, p. 301.

¹⁵ John A. Price, "Migration and Adaptation of American Indians to Los Angeles," *Human Organization*, Vol. 27, No. 2, (summer, 1968), p. 171.

¹⁶ One factor of great importance was the close association of powerful Metis families (such as the McKays and the Sinclairs) with the administration of the reserves in the first generation after the treaties. The descendants of Bernard Constand, for example, directly relate the half-breed farm instructor with the sale of land in the James Smith Reserve in 1903. A consortium of farmers, including a medical doctor from Prince Albert, apparently was in close touch with the instructor who managed to bring off the deal *(Interviews*, April, 1970). At the same time, the registered Indians expressed considerable dislike of the half-breeds clustered on the fringes of the reserve – shadowy go-betweens in the white-Indian universe.

[17] *The Financial Post*, October 8, 1966; January 4, 1969.

[18] *Saskatoon Star-Phoenix*, November 21, 1967.

[19] Other examples similarly reveal the intimidating effect of white control of native organizations. In one case, the above-mentioned New Jersey couple dropped in on a native group struggling to debate an issue in a more or less systematic way. The effect was devastating. They took over the meeting, wrote an agenda, and chaired it. The Indians and Metis fell silent for the rest of the evening, and some withdrew altogether from the group.

[20] *Hawthorn Report*, Vol. 2, p. 109ff.

[21] Among others, Ablon, "Relocated American Indians in the San Francisco Bay Area," *op. cit.*, p. 297.

[22] *Saskatoon Star-Phoenix*, November 5, 1969. Actually, the board of directors was defunct.

[23] This is not to say that the agencies necessarily employ these powers, but they are there as a threat at all times, and they deeply affect the attitudes of the Indian and Metis toward life in the city.

[24] *The Indian News*, Vol. 10, No. 4, December, 1967.

[25] See Ablon, "Relocated American Indians in the San Francisco Bay Area," *op. cit.*, p. 301.

[26] *Hawthorn Report*, Vol. 1, p. 362.

# 9
## A Strategy of Change and Participation

### The Dimensions of Poverty

There are no "solutions" to Indian poverty in Canadian cities – that is the problem. The majority, the *Welfare*, are internal exiles without hope and aspiration. They live in a world which has rejected them from the beginning – their version of the winning of the West. Our civilization was born and reared at an enormous cost to the "first Canadians." Indian poverty more than any other is a symptom of the limitations of our society. Or to express it another way, having broken the Indians, our society must now accept the consequences.

A first step has been to diagnose the problem. To summarize, the present system of relations between whites and Indians in the city raises four distinct sets of problems.

1. Indians are poor. As a minority group they do not have adequate housing, health, education and levels of incomes, and they get more than their share of degrading work when there is work at all. In the city, as on the reserve (or in their Northern communities), Indians and Metis are beyond the Welfare State, beyond history. The deadening routine of poverty is maintained from one generation to the next.

Moreover, there is no indication that things are getting better for the Indians. The educational level is slowly rising, but so is that of the larger society. Indians are being placed in more jobs, but it is not certain that they are holding them. But even if they did, the surge in population each year places increasing numbers of employable native people on the job market. Hard-core poverty in Canada cannot be broken by appealing to the virtues of self-help and there is no automatic economic mechanism which

176

will eradicate it. The case of the Indians demonstrates how prosperity and relatively full employment can leave a derelict population behind. If anything, the increasing technological sophistication of Canadian industry will render the position of the Indian urban poor that much more hopeless.

The "Indian Problem" seen from the perspective of hard-core poverty is part of the broader issue facing the country. However, it is significant that the public attention it has received for nearly a decade has not broken the urban poverty cycle. New programs were called into existence; much enthusiasm was aroused in the larger society. For part of this period the economy was functioning well; later it began to falter. But the point is that Indians and Metis remain the most deprived minority in Canada.

2.  Indians and Metis are at a political disadvantage in Canada. Hard-core poverty particularly in the case of the Indians, can only be met by political action. This follows from the inability of economic growth in Canada to alleviate deprivation. But to act politically, a group must be able to bargain, and that means developing organizational strength. For reasons which I have given, there are tremendous obstacles in the city to the uniting of the Indians and Metis behind a stable leadership. Although some factors result from the unique historical treatment of the native people in Canada, others refer rather simply to the state of poverty itself: people who are broken and in skid row, or people who subsist at a poverty level and are dependent on welfare caretakers, have no political muscle. Again this is a general criticism of the political system, not specific to the native minority. It would hold even if all Indians wanted or were in a position, to assimilate.

Indians and Metis share another political impediment with the hard-core poor: they have few friends and many enemies. All the evidence to the contrary, Indians are upbraided for their demands for money and for special privileges, for taxing the average Canadian dry. Conservatives of all stands, therefore, can rally against the poor and the Indians as lacking initiative and collecting welfare in taxis. But it is not even clear if Indian and Metis have much *solid* support in the more reflective middle class and working class sectors of the country. The former group has done the most to sustain interest in Indian problems in the last decade but there are now definite signs of attrition. The mass media in particular are now bored as the intractability of native poverty has become clearer. We can now expect a series of exposés on corruption within Indian organizations as a first method of debunking the movement.

The University may serve as a continuing catalyst for enquiries into the mechanisms of urban Indian poverty. This is a mixed blessing since it inevitably entails social science surveys that native people find objectionable. That price may not be too high if it maintains a public focus on the subject. One of the most disturbing features of the Canadian public is its fickle shifting from one issue to the next. The greatest danger now is that the Indians will lose the public interest which has so far been their most important political weapon. However uncritical the public may have been in the last decade, and however insufficient the efforts made, without that broad support Indian leaders would have been able to accomplish far less.

The Canadian working class, for its part, has little to say about the Indians and is not a source of reliable support. It is significant that the Saskatchewan pro-labour CCF was far less willing to assist the native people than the business-oriented Liberty Party headed by Ross Thatcher.

In the end, only Ottawa can set the pace in Indian Affairs, and this means that the Liberal and Conservative Parties must be willing to face the Canadian poverty issue in general and the specific problem of Indian poverty. So far the Trudeau government has simply not done this; nothing suggests that the Conservative Party could do any better. There are not enough Indian votes. There is at least an even chance that Ottawa will evade its responsibilities and fritter away the opportunities for reform that do exist.

3. The Indian minority in the city, and the Indians as a group in Canadian society, are unique. "Special status" is a fact of life, not a legal and administrative nicety. It will remain whether they remain ground down in poverty or whether they creatively redefine relations with white society. But present poverty programs aim at assimilation in a continuing fruitless attempt to deny Indianness. Decision-making is centred almost exclusively in the bureaucracies, eliminating the expression of demands from the native community.

By denying Indians any control over their lives and by rejecting their birthright, the poverty programs remove any moral incentive to escape poverty. They are sterile exchanges of money for more or less good behaviour; they are not aimed at mobilizing the anger and creativity of the native minority. Nor can they as they are now structured. For unless Indians are turned into "proper little brown men," as one Indian leader put it, the bureaucracies will not tolerate them. After a century, it is still the case that white society is determined to isolate and destroy the culture of the indigenous population. Not only is it favoured in every way – power, wealth, language, religion – but it must also keep in check any form of Indian revival, which alone will make a dent in urban poverty.

Among Blacks in the United States, the revival of nativist movements, sometimes (as in the case of the Muslims) based on traditional religions, has been a potent force for rejuvenation.[1] Whatever the specific direction chosen by the Indians of Canada, and that can only be their decision, the problem of identity is fundamental to an attack on poverty. Unless the native people can work out for themselves a context for their moral, material, and cultural advancement within the Canadian setting, little can be accomplished. So far Pan-Indianism is merely a symptom that change is necessary – specific strategies must now be produced. One thing is absolutely clear however – a policy of assimilation perpetuates and enlarges skid row.

The maintenance of the reserves is central to Indian revival. Although small and isolated, they remain the single most important aspect of urbanization. They remain "home" for urban migrants, and ensure the possibility at least of going back. The institutions of the reserve and their continuing role in the lives of Indians, render the urbanization process of Indians distinct from any other group in Canada. The potential for the moral rejuvenation of the reserves is immense. Should the main recommendations of Ottawa's *White Paper* of July, 1969 be implemented, in effect "terminating" the special status of Indians, the reserves will be lost, and the native people will be permanently pauperized, a skid row sub-culture. It would be an incomparable disaster for Indians; and ominous for Canadian cities.

If, however, the reserves are saved, Indians will retain a base of operations and the opportunity for social experimentation. As indicated, few Indian reserves and Metis communities, given their location and resource inadequacies, offer prospects for escaping almost complete dependence on the white-controlled economy. But as self-government on Indian reserves increases, the native leadership may develop effective programs designed to re-assert Indianness in Canada.

The urban situation is more complex, for the same base of operations does not exist. Indians can return to the reserve at will, but this flexibility does not solve problems. It merely reinforces the uniqueness of Indian migration patterns as opposed to other ethnic groups, and the urgency of new strategies.

4. The analysis of the Indian urban social system showed that the major groupings, the *Affluent*, the *Anomic* and the *Welfare*, exhibit different needs in the urban environment. They share a common sense of Indianness, but not a common set of expectations. They see themselves existing as a people distinct from the white majority; but common consciousness has produced no common plan to improve their social and economic positions in Canada. In the absence of Indian solidarity in the city, the design of urban poverty programs remains based on the Canadian experience with European immigrant populations. Unfortunately, this experience is not relevant to the Indian case. The latter case is far more complex. Not unnaturally, the result so far has been unimpressive.

## The Choice of Priorities

The present study has underlined the very considerable efforts of the agencies concerned with Indian and Metis migration to the city; in particular, it has stressed the fact that they are not effective. The central reason for failure is less a lack of goodwill than bad planning. Unless the poverty programs shift their priorities and unless they develop new concepts that transcend the settler experience and experiment with new structures, they will continue to fail.

In terms of the native urban stratification system, the poverty programs assist only the top and bottom strata. In neither case are efforts "wasted" as such. Assisting the *Affluent* to solidify a prestigious position in urban society ensures the protection of at least one segment, however small, of the Indian-Metis population of Canada. Extending assistance to *Welfare* Indians and Metis increases their meagre incomes and brings many out of the reserves and the Northern communities into contact with the urban environment.

Whether these objectives are the most urgent remains a moot point. The *type* of assistance and support to the *Affluent* contributes to the political malfunctioning of the Indian-Metis community in the city. The dole extended to the *Welfare* unquestionably is fostering the growth of skid row. The chief effect, in fact, of the mass of official and voluntary welfare programs is to make life in the city a little more attractive than it might be on the reserve. But only just a little. The poverty programs do not affect the deadening cycle of poverty, the institutions of poverty that render the problem so intractable. This is particularly the case with voluntary agencies that have an emotional commitment to poverty. In the long run, it is surely unwise to stimulate deliberately the growth of Indian skid rows. Unless there is some likelihood of effective programs attacking not merely a symptom, but the entire problem, the present strategy is a counsel of despair.

Any attempt to alleviate Indian poverty in Canadian cities must recognize the totality of the problem. A *long-range* plan must aim at changing the existing institutions which condemn not only Indians but millions of other Canadians to a life of deprivation. A *short-term* thrust must deal with distortions of a less profound character, where immediate gains can be foreseen. Both approaches must go together but it is essential that they be distinguished to ensure effectiveness and to guard against dissension among reformers. Radical reform necessitates careful planning in the short run, just as incremental change loses its meaning if not related to basic structural change. Absurd as Indian suffering may be in a country as rich as Canada, it will not go away by invoking Louis Riel or Karl Marx.

No person knowledgeable in the field of Indian poverty in Canadian cities would presume that the *Welfare* grouping can be decisively assisted in the short run. Housing, employment, education, the environment in which it lives, would have to be altered to create a viable alternative to skid row. Above all, the success of any strategy with this group will depend on forms of nativist nationalism that must stem from the Indian-Metis community itself. In turn, the economic and cultural revival of the native population will have to be integrated into a general scheme encompassing not only the cities, but the reserves and Northern communities as well.

Massive community development may yield gradual results. The mechanisms involved – the role of Indian organizations as opposed to official agencies, and the strategy to be adopted in each case – remain as yet unclear. The only certain thing is that we are years away from such an effort. There is little evidence as yet that Canadians are prepared for the responsibility of managing their own resources or curbing their appetite for consumer goods.

In this situation, the provision of a minimum income to all Canadians, including Indians, and massive support for Indian reserves and communities appear the most realistic long-term goals in reducing the chaos of the poverty programs. The many agencies now operating in the welfare field not only have a vested interest in maintaining their clientele, but they also reinforce a Caretaker-Client power relationship that prevents any initiative from below. Simply sweeping away much of the welfare superstructure would permit far more funding for the Indians, and it would help undermine the patterns of dependence of the reserve background.

Primary attention should be given to the *Anomic*. In terms of aspirations and realistic possibilities for successful adaptation, the *Anomic* represent the segment of the native social structures most in need of assistance. They have a desire and a will to adapt in the urban environment. Although they do not comprise a majority of the Indian-Metis minority, their success or failure marks the crucial difference between the creation of a sizeable adjusted native community in the city, and the unchecked growth of an urban *Welfare* native population.

Again I make the point: saving the *Anomic* Indians from downward mobility into the ranks of the *Welfare* is not a panacea for the entire Indian problem. We fool ourselves to think that the misdeeds of generations can be corrected through official programs. The first step is to raise at least one group beyond the level of the *Affluent* Indians and Metis in the city.

## The Dilemma of Innovation for the Anomic

A prominent Indian leader once remarked that:

> There must be a revolution in the minds of white people to break down the barriers, the misconceptions, the bigotry and the racism. Do the white people want us continually to rely on Welfare with a bare existence? Do they want us to live in squalor so that we can continue to fulfil psychological needs of white do-gooders who feel they are glorifying God by sending us seconds?[2]

What, however, does that mean in the real world, where as we have seen in the urban environment, the Indian-Metis minority is utterly dependent and without room for maneuver? The latest and most simple-minded neo-liberal argument counsels a policy of caution: let us bad whites do nothing, for social engineering has emasculated the Indian and increased the wretchedness of his condition; let us wait for the Indians to speak, and then we shall support "representative Indian organizations" offering only assistance that they desire.[3]

How pious, and indeed how true. But how unfortunately irrelevant. First, the discussion of the native urban organizational capacity suggests that native groups are presently incapable of designing or effectively implementing urban poverty programs. Second, and more serious, the stratification system leaves the *Anomic* in an impossibly weak position *vis-à-vis* the *Affluent*; and the *Affluent* have little in common with, nor do they appear to be very concerned about, their native brothers. Certainly we have arrived at a time when there is no substitute for native leadership in an urban organization, or in any other, for that matter. A revived Indian consciousness will no longer tolerate white leadership and control at this level. In the case of the *Anomic*, however, institutional reform must precede the emergence of native leadership. This group is so effectively controlled, so completely dependent, and so totally without power contacts in the larger society that the spontaneous emergence of a leadership from its ranks is precluded.

If social action programs rather than bureaucratic services are required for an effective strategy, it is sheer nonsense to recommend inaction until that group develops a leadership cadre. Unless the bureaucracies are pried apart and alternatives prepared, the cadre will never emerge, much less survive. In the absence of native leadership, the role of white supporters is to *open alternatives for potential leaders* who can develop in an environment free of terror and dependency. Only whites and Indians working together can attack the central problem of Indian migration to the cities. Native impetus and drive must coincide with intelligent funding and technical assistance.

## The Indian Enclave in the Urban Environment

A well-designed, self-governing, native, residential community inside the city is one concept which could meet many of the requirements of the urban *Anomic* Indians and Metis. Provided it was carefully designed and assisted, the urban Indian enclave might rally the energies and enthusiasm of this grouping. Several authors appear to be moving independently toward an endorsement of this policy position:

> A very few carefully selected nuclear family groups who are related and whose economic situation creates an incentive toward economic improvement, might be placed in a reasonably good urban neighbourhood. This district might consist of home-owners rather than renters, people who were self-conscious about gardening and keeping up their properties. The newcomers could be helped to obtain jobs and perceptively helped to find their way in the new setting. If some of them succeeded and their children succeeded in the community and school, the effect of this would be multiple among their home band members.[4]

Similarly, the concept of neighbourhood control has been advocated with reference to Blacks in American cities:

> We think of the political sub-system of society as involving the executive, legislative and judicial branches of government which operate at the national, state and local levels. In our view, a new level of government which should be given increased responsibility, autonomy and power is the neighbourhood.[5]

Although with a different structure and relationship with urban institutions, an Indian enclave for the *Anomic* Indian and Metis migrants would provide these families and individuals with the community support that many other ethnic groups developed to cushion the shock of urbanization. Native people might choose to live in one area, or they might live dispersed, although centred around a common set of community institutions and services, designed specifically for the economic, social and psychological needs of the *Anomic* segment.

*Economic.* All authors agree that the Indians and Metis must have increased employment opportunities provided by the larger society. Given the complexity of the employment market, no attempt should be made to duplicate government services. The contribution of the neighbourhood association would lie in more effective communication and liaison with existing agencies, and in assisting heads of households to maintain work habits and motivation.

*Psychological.* Assistance would be provided in liberating the *Anomic* Indians and Metis from the psychological dilemma of the culture clash situation. The enclave would allow the *Anomic* to safeguard a racial heritage different from that of the larger society, and to construct meaningful alternatives that respond to the historical imperatives of a widely different cultural tradition and a heritage of conflict with the settler culture.[6] It would decentralize decision-making, restore power to the community which has long been usurped by the bureaucracies, and thereby foster a socio-political capacity that would strengthen native institutions and deepen the participation of the Indian-Metis minority in city life. It would place the group in a situation where it would have a possibility of influencing the outcome of important decisions in the bargaining process.

The community might include a day-care centre for working mothers, as well as educational, cultural and home-visiting services operating in close cooperation with existing government programs. In this environment Canada Manpower upgrading and training projects might succeed.

*Social.* Most important, the native enclave would create a community for the *Anomic* which would compensate for the disabilities of their positions in the kinship structure. Billingsley has suggested a social system approach to the study of Negro family life. According to his argument, the Black family includes within itself several sub-systems; these interact with the individual sub-systems of the Negro community, which in turn are embedded in the major institutions of the larger society that set the conditions for Negro family life.[7]

It is very useful to conceptualize the needs of *Anomic* Indians and Metis in a similar fashion. Contrasted with the *Affluent*, the *Anomic* family has support neither from the Indian-Metis community, nor from the wider society. Family life on the reserve assisted the *Affluent* in developing stable nuclear families buttressed by carefully-controlled extended family relationships. When the *Anomic* migrate to the city, they must battle their extended families while coping with other impediments such as finding employment despite low educational and skill levels, budgeting on small incomes, and adapting to rigorous time schedules.

The Indian enclave would draw together into a protected environment the families who cannot by themselves master these multiple obstacles to successful adaptation. Living together in a self-governing community, their values would be mutually reinforcing, and they could draw strength from the knowledge and friendship of families in a similar situation. Counselling, where necessary, would be carried on by other members or by trained native personnel under community supervision.

The enclave would create in the city the socialization experience that the *Affluent* had as a result of their leading status on the reserves. Moreover, as a community with a stake in survival and in its linkages with the complementary institutions of the larger society, the *Anomic* would be in a position to control the influx of relatives and thus to protect their home economies. The leadership of the community would carefully select Indian and Metis applicants from different reserves and communities and help them construct a new Pan-Indian identity in the city. Excluded from the *Affluent*, the *Anomic* need a continually reinforcing atmosphere to enable them to build the necessary toughness for dealing with the larger society. The community would be the mechanism for fostering the development of this discipline. No pressure would be exercised upon families to dispense with common facilities until they could cope with day-to-day problems on their own without the fear of failure.

The families involved would be entirely free to take advantage of existing programs offered by Indian and Metis associations. The major responsibility of the self-governing enclave would be to develop and administer only those programs and activities which would enhance both the structure and functioning of the family among the residents of the community, and the physical, social and emotional well-being of their children.

### Requirements

1. Assurance must be given that the project would have adequate maintenance and not degenerate into that which it is being designed to prevent, i.e., a slum.

2. The City Council should be represented in some way on the Indian Board responsible for the operation of the community.

3. The project should provide a symbol of pride to the entire Indian community. It should "fill the cultural gap" and provide incentives to participate in the larger community.

4. The design of the major structures and facilities should reflect significant aspects of Indian tradition, both in terms of architecture and land use.

5. The Indians should formulate the policies for the operation of the community.

6. The Indians should choose a leader or leaders to represent the community in the City Council and to head a Committee on Urbanization to coordinate the planning of the many agencies in the city, now acting in isolation from each other and often at cross-purposes.

7. Advisory and legal services should be available to help administer the complex, to direct its construction, and to train personnel where necessary.

8. The project should have low rentals.

9. The project should be close to schools and other urban facilities.

10. In the fields of education and housing it would be essential that existing off-reserve programs be stepped up to accommodate members who feel that they are ready to move into general city housing, *provided that they want to leave the community* after adaptation to the urban environment.

## Stages of Growth and Administrative Structures

1. A first necessary step would be the consolidation of the various native organizations and the formation of a study group.

2. A Directorship would then be formed, including representatives from the City Council, the IMB, the Federation of Saskatchewan Indians, the IAB, and the private sector. It would carry out an extensive survey of the main "feeder" reserves and communities around each city. An Advisory Board would include city, business and governmental participants.

Subject to the final authority of the Board, the members of the community would elect a Community Development Director.

Specifically, he would chair a Committee on Urbanization dealing with the coordination of the various agencies' programs involving Indian migration. The Director would have responsibility for selecting individuals and families from the reserves and northern communities and recommending them to the Board. His role would therefore be of extreme importance. In general, it is expected that the Director would have aldermanic status acting as the spokesman for the native population in the city.

## Conclusion

The development of a strong and adjusted native urban minority depends on the successful dovetailing of two strategies. The first, the provision of expanded opportunities, depends on the initiation by the larger society of expanded programs in education, housing and employment, to foster economic and socio-political modernization. Resources must be made available by white organizations – the fact of dependency defines the position of the native population in Canadian society. Greater resources, however, are not enough. A second strategy, the stimulation of alternatives, is essential to develop urban native institutions which can create a social, cultural and political infrastructure for the utilization of inputs from the outside. Local involvement and control are not mere aspects but decisive ingredients of modernization. Logic, humanity and self-interest demand immediate attention to the latter dimension in the urban environment.

[1] See for example, E. U. Essien-Udoun, *Black Nationalism: A Search for Identity in America*, Chicago and London, University of Chicago Press, 1962.

[2] "Interview with Harold Cardinal," *Maclean's*, December, 1966, p. 20.

[3] Edgar S. Cahn, *Our Brother's Keeper: The Indian in White America*, New York and Cleveland, New Community Press, 1969, p. 190.

[4] R. Dunning, "Some Aspects of Indian Policy and Administration," *Anthropologica*, Vol. 4, Nov. 1962.

[5] Andrew Billingsley, *Black Families in White America*, Englewood Cliffs, Prentice-Hall, 1968, pp. 176-177.

[6] Compare Billingsley, *op. cit.*, p. 189.

[7] *Ibid.*, p. 5.

# Index

191